Born in Market Harborough in 1
in the RAF and ran his own ta
company from scratch and then walking away with an eight-figure sum. Since then, he has built a portfolio of more than 50 properties across the UK, co-owns Corby Town FC and holds majority shares in several start-ups. He also coaches founders and CEOs.

POWER THROUGH

A JOURNEY FROM PRISON TO SUCCESS

JAMES LONGLEY

Published in 2025
by Eye Books Ltd
29A Barrow Street
Much Wenlock
Shropshire
TF13 6EN

www.eye-books.com

ISBN: 9781785633560

Cover design by Ifan Bates
Typeset in Garamond and Davidas

British Library Cataloguing in Publication Data
A catalogue record for this book is available from the British Library.

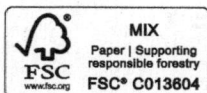

MIX
Paper | Supporting
responsible forestry
FSC
www.fsc.org   FSC® C013604

Our authorised representative in the EU for product safety is:
Logos Europe, 9 rue Nicolas Poussin, 17000, La Rochelle, France
contact@logoseurope.eu

CONTENTS

The events and conversations in this book are accurate to the best of the author's ability, although some names and details have been changed to protect the privacy of others.

1

SENT DOWN

As I PACED ANXIOUSLY around the crowded foyer of Leicester Crown Court waiting for my solicitor, I caught sight of the taxi driver I'd hit. I hesitated, then walked over to him.

'Sorry, mate,' I said.

'Okay,' he murmured

'You know, it wasn't racist.'

'Okay,' he repeated, and shook my hand.

I don't know if he believed me, but it hadn't been a racist attack. I'd ended up in a fight with him in the early hours of the morning, not because he was Asian but because he had stopped the taxi in the middle of nowhere and refused to take me home to Market Harborough unless I gave him more money, claiming the can of Coke I'd spilt had damaged the passenger seat. As I was drunk, my recollections were hazy.

When my solicitor arrived, I said, 'How do you think it's likely to go?'

'It's hard to say,' he replied. 'But if you've had community service before and completed it, then there's a good chance, if you're found guilty, that the judge may recommend it rather than prison as a punishment.'

'Yeah?' I said, hopefully.

Around the same time as the incident with the taxi driver, I'd been found guilty of being in possession of fake currency and given a community service order. This might make me sound like I was a perpetual criminal, but I wasn't. I'd hit the taxi driver in a moment of drunken anger, and I was found with fake currency because, stupidly, I had taken it to help ease my financial problems.

'That happens sometimes,' said the solicitor. 'By the way, a different barrister has been appointed to represent you.'

'Why's that?'

He shrugged.

The barrister arrived at 9.30am, looking flustered. The court case was due to begin at 10am. She briskly introduced herself and ushered me into a room.

'Right, I've read the case notes,' she said, matter-of-factly.

'Okay,' I said.

'I don't know what you might be thinking, but you're going to be found guilty and you're going to be sent to prison.'

'Hang on! What do you mean?'

'You've admitted to assaulting the taxi driver, multiple witnesses say they saw you assault him, and one of them says you used a racial slur.'

'But I didn't hit him because he was Asian.'

'I'm sorry, Mr Longley, but I have to say I think the jury are going to find you guilty.'

'You mentioned prison.'

'That's right. You might go to prison for a couple of years.'

'A couple of years!' I couldn't take this in.

She smiled thinly. 'That's the worst-case scenario. If you plead guilty, you'll get credit for that. And then we can talk about your RAF career, your daughter, university and so on, and you might get off with community service.'

'So, you're saying I should plead guilty?'

'That's my advice based on my experience of these sorts of cases. The racial element of this case makes it more serious.'

'I wasn't expecting this.'

'I'm sorry, but I think in these circumstances you have to plead guilty.'

She told me I would have to make my mind up quickly, and left me in the room to think about it. I didn't want to plead guilty, but if it meant avoiding a prison sentence, then I would have to.

When I was called to enter the court room, I stepped forward feeling anxious. An usher motioned me towards the dock. The jury hadn't been sworn in yet. My barrister informed the judge that I wanted to change my plea. A brief conversation ensued between the two of them and the prosecution barrister. In the end the judge nodded. He asked me how I pleaded to the charges of assault occasioning actual bodily harm and racially aggravated assault occasioning actual bodily harm. 'Guilty,' I replied. The judge then adjourned the case for a pre-sentencing report.

I left the court room with my head spinning. My life no longer felt within my control. With the threat of prison hanging over me, my emotions were in turmoil.

My barrister explained that a pre-sentencing report was an expert assessment of the nature and causes of an offender's behaviour and the risk they pose, as well as an independent recommendation of the sentencing options available to the court.

'What's the point of it?' I asked.

'It provides the court with a greater understanding of the background and the context of the offending behaviour, rather than just the details of the offence,' she said.

A few days later, I had a meeting with a probation officer at Wigston, just outside Leicester. He interviewed me about the case and told me I should contact the RAF and the University of Northampton for references.

'Do you have any Asian friends?' he asked.

'Yeah,' I said.

'Do you think any of them will provide character references for you and state that they have never seen you behave in a racist way?'

'I guess so.'

'Good. That might help your case.'

My barrister phoned me the following week. She said the pre-sentencing report had recommended community service.

'That's brilliant news,' I said.

'It is, but the judge isn't bound by it.'

'You mean he could still give me a prison sentence?'

'I'm afraid so. But a community service recommendation is very positive.'

I tried to put the case out of my mind and carry on as normal with my life, but it was hard to do. I just wanted to go to crown court and get it over and done with, so I could move on with my life.

Eventually, I received a letter telling me the date of the sentencing. It had been set for 22 May 2003, a year after the incident. I hired a solicitor and he engaged a barrister to represent me. He told me the barrister would be given all the case notes. I was so worried in the run-up to my appearance, I found it hard to sleep. I used to go for runs around the playing field at the back of the leisure centre and then lie down on the grass because I was so tired. I'd wake up half an hour later.

On the appointed date, I returned to Leicester Crown Court for sentencing at 10am. On the one hand, I was relieved that the day had finally arrived. I told myself that it might be all over in a couple of hours, and I'd just get community service. On the other hand, I was petrified that I might be sent to prison.

When I was summoned into court, I nervously made my way to the dock. The judge stared at me and said, 'I accept the offence was entirely out of character and I also accept that the assault in this case did not have as its prime motivation racial prejudice of any kind. It is a great shame to see someone of your background in the dock.'

My spirits lifted. I was going to get a community service order.

The judge continued: 'However, taxi drivers are entitled to the protection of this court. I've considered the case carefully, and I've decided that I have to give a custodial sentence. I'm not sure how long this should be yet. I'm going to think about it over lunch. In the meantime, I'm remanding you in custody until 2pm.'

I was taken down to the cells. My barrister came in and said, 'Look, I'm not saying this is going to happen, but I've seen it before where a judge tries to make a defendant worried that he's going to prison and then changes their mind.'

'Yeah?' I said.

'As I say, sometimes this happens.'

Her words gave me some hope. I was in a cell with a guy who was going to be sentenced for sexual assault. We both sat there in silence, each in our own private world, staring at the floor.

I was taken back up to the court room just before 2pm. I was shaking when I entered the dock, where two prison officers were standing.

The judge said, 'Having weighed up the case carefully, I have decided to give you a custodial sentence of eight months.'

I waited for the judge to add that he was suspending the sentence, which meant I wouldn't have to go to prison; but no more words came. I really was going to jail for eight months. I stood there, utterly stunned, feeling like I had just taken a major punch in the stomach. My mum and dad were with my partner, Sally, on the other side of the courtroom, but I couldn't look at any of them as I reeled from the sentence. In any case, there was barely time to look at anyone, because the judge was already telling the prison officers to take me down to the cells.

One of them took me by the arm. 'This way,' he said in a low voice. He said it kindly, and when we got down below, he shrugged his surprise at me, as if to say he hadn't been expecting a custodial sentence either.

But there was no arguing. I was about to go to prison, something that would lead me to question the way the criminal justice system worked, as well as changing my life in ways I could never possibly have foreseen.

2

BRAVE JAMES

My EARLIEST MEMORY is from when I was five, and my dad took me in his blue Vauxhall Cavalier to see Leicester City play Manchester United. I don't recall anything about the game, apart from the deafening noise and the huge, tightly packed crowd, but I do remember that Gary Lineker was playing for Leicester. And, no doubt, he scored.

I was born at Leicester Royal Infirmary on 11 September 1976. My mother was just twenty-one. She named me James because she had liked the name after watching David Essex play a character called Jim in the film *That'll Be the Day*. She remembers a nurse opening the windows because it was so hot, so one of the first sounds I probably heard was the chants of Leicester City supporters at Filbert Street.

My dad grew up in Leicester. His father, who had served in the army, moved there from Yorkshire. My dad had two brothers and a sister who had Down Syndrome; she died at the age of thirty.

My mum was born in Market Harborough. Her parents split up when she was young, and her dad moved to Cornwall. When she was thirteen her mum died, so she ended up living with her granny.

My parents met in 1971 at the Palais de Danse in Leicester. After getting married in 1974, they rented a flat in the city before buying a house in Logan Street in Market Harborough. In 1977 they moved less than a mile away to a house on Lubenham Hill.

Market Harborough is a small town about fifteen miles south of Leicester and close to the Northamptonshire border. Locals just call it Harborough. Its most notable features are St Dionysius Church with its tall spire: a seventeenth-century timber-framed building on wooden pillars that was once the grammar school; and the red-brick Symington factory, which made corsets for retailers such as Marks and Spencer. When my parents moved there, it contained the kind of independent shops you found in many small towns, along with a Woolworths, Boots and Burton's. Champers Café in the Square was a popular place to grab something to eat or have a cup of tea, and my mum often met her friends there. To the north of the town was the basin of the Leicester Line of the Grand Union Canal, lined by a number of old warehouses. If you ever bought a packet of Golden Wonder crisps, you would know from the back of the packet that the company's head office was in Market Harborough, on Abbey Street.

When I was seven, we moved to a three-bedroom house in Cromwell Crescent, on the south side of the River Welland. By now I had a younger brother called Tom and a sister, Debbie. I shared a bedroom with Tom, and we had lots of fights, as brothers are prone to do, but overall we got on pretty well and played football together most days. Apparently my first words were 'outside' and 'football'.

I went to Fairfield Road Primary School for a year and then to Farndon Fields Primary School. I don't remember much about my primary school days, but when I was six, I saw a boy called Paul attack one of the teachers, Mrs White, in class one day. Since that memory sticks out, it must have left a lasting impression.

My mum's dad lived in St Ives in Cornwall. When I was seven and Tom was five, my parents took us to Victoria Coach Station in London and put us on a National Express coach to Cornwall. In those days, a hostess was provided for unaccompanied children. The coach travelled through the night and we were met by my grandad at Penzance, where he was a traffic warden and his wife helped run an ice-cream shop near the pier. One day Tom and I went to the end of the pier and watched some older lads jumping off it into the water, so we did the same. When my grandad discovered what had happened, he wasn't happy. I think we were a bit of a handful for him. When he took us to a Radio 1 road show, we got lost in the crowds. After he found us, he gave us both a smack for getting lost. We never stayed with him again.

Another summer, my parents took us to stay in a caravan in Dorset. I recall that Tom and I clambered up Durdle Door, a natural limestone arch in the sea near Lulworth, unaware of how dangerous this was. We had no fear.

Usually when we went on holiday, though, it was to Butlin's in Minehead or to stay with Mum's family in Devon or Cornwall – but we had plenty of days out to places like Skegness or Hunstanton too. My mum and dad would pack the car and then watch the weather to decide where to go. My dad liked cycling. On one occasion, he set off for Skegness at 5am, and we caught up with him later in the car and picked him up. When I think back to those summer holidays, I just remember eating fish and chips and sheltering under an umbrella from the pouring rain.

My mum and dad promised to buy me a dog when I was eight if I did better at school, especially with my handwriting. I really wanted a dog, so I began to pay more attention to the teachers and try harder. My parents kept their promise and bought me a springer spaniel, which I called Twinkle because of the way the stars twinkled in the sky.

My favourite TV programme when I was small was *The Muppets*. I always got very excited when it came on, and I even had an album with all the songs from the show.

I don't recall much else about my early years, yet beyond sleepy Market Harborough significant events were taking place. Margaret Thatcher became prime minister, Britain went to war with Argentina to reclaim the Falkland Islands, the Troubles in Northern Ireland were at their peak, there was a national miners' strike to try to prevent the closure of the collieries and, internationally, the USA and the Soviet Union were locked in the Cold War. As a child, of course, these sorts of things don't make much sense to you; they are all part of the adult world.

My dad worked for several years at Tungstone, the battery maker, one of the largest employers in the town. It had two sites: a factory in Lathkill Street, off Northampton Road, and a warehouse near the railway station. He had also been a milkman with Kirby & West. When I was about ten, he would take me out on the float with him. One morning, he asked me if I wanted to have a go at driving it. 'Yes!' I shrieked. I got behind the wheel, carefully pressed the pedal and set off down the street, only to crash the float into the railings in front of

Robert Smyth School. My dad jumped out. 'Quick!' he said. 'Help me fix these before anyone sees us.' We managed to push the railings back together, then drove away.

My mum had various jobs when I was growing up, such as working as a barmaid in the Peacock pub in St Mary's Place and as a secretary in a solicitor's office.

We would have fish and chips on Thursdays, because that was when my dad got paid, and a roast on Sundays. We weren't a poor family, but money was tight. I remember eating jam sandwiches a lot. My mum and dad didn't go out that much. They just worked hard to look after three kids and two dogs.

Apart from my dad, we all had a problem with our weight. Back then we weren't aware of 'the calories in, calories out' formula with which most people are familiar nowadays. We ate far too much because we all liked large plates of food. I'd go into town and have a cob and a cake from Wesses Bakery and think nothing of it. I wouldn't dream of having a cake at lunchtime now. When I look at photos of myself in the football team back then, I'm always the biggest. Needless to say, some of the kids at primary school ribbed me about my weight.

At one point, my mum, who was only five foot seven, went up to eighteen stone. She eventually joined Weight Care, which is similar to Weight Watchers, and came second in Slimmer of the Year, losing eight stone. Later, in the late eighties, she trained to be an instructor and ran her own aerobics and slimming classes in a church hall. Long before that, she began to weigh us all each week on the bathroom scales, and she'd get upset if we'd put weight on. I started losing weight around the age of thirteen. I don't know why it happened. Maybe it was because I got taller. I know it wasn't because I went on a diet; that would never have occurred to me. Whatever the reason,

I'm pleased to say I've managed to keep it off ever since.

Christmas was always an exciting time. My mum would leave a mince pie and a glass of sherry for Santa on Christmas Eve. I'd wake up early, go downstairs and see all the presents under the tree. My mum would cook a great Christmas dinner, and we would usually go to my grandma's in Leicester on Boxing Day. Sometimes my dad would take me to see Leicester play.

I remember my mum saying to me one year, 'Santa doesn't exist, James.' I then told Tom and Debbie what she'd said, even though Mum asked me to keep it a secret. They never let on for ages that they knew. One Christmas, my parents bought a half-size snooker table for me and Tom. We spent hours playing on it in the dining room. My dad sometimes took us to play snooker at two social clubs, known as the 'top club' and the 'bottom club'.

Market Harborough didn't have a cinema. If we went to see a film it would be at the ABC or the Odeon in Leicester. The first films I remember seeing were *ET*, *Rocky IV* and the *Star Wars* trilogy. My grandparents on my dad's side lived in Leicester, and we'd often go to visit them on a Saturday. A big treat was to go to Grimsby Fisheries on Welford Road for fish and chips; the portions were huge.

After leaving primary school, I went to Welland Park College secondary school until I was fourteen and then to Robert Smyth School, which had previously been known as Market Harborough Grammar School and could trace its roots to that old timber-framed building in the centre of the town.

At Welland Park I started arranging boxing matches at lunchtime in the cloakroom. I'd persuade one of the other lads to referee and then two others would put on boxing gloves and throw punches at each other. I once fought a lad called Jason, who thought he was quite tough. He didn't like the fact that

I was getting the better of him, so he flung his gloves away, broke a leg off a chair and chased me around the school. That wasn't the first run-in I'd had with him. He'd tried to bully me because I was overweight (back in the days before I slimmed down). A couple of other lads did the same. One time, one of them kneed me in the balls, which really hurt, but I stood up to all of them.

At school, I messed about a lot in class, but my dad instilled in me from an early age the value of working hard – 'If you want something, you have to work for it' – and I took his words seriously when it came to my out-of-school hours. By the age of eleven, I was doing paper rounds on my red Raleigh bike for Monty, an old man who ran a newsagent on Bath Street. I did a paper round before school, an afternoon round, with the *Leicester Mercury*, after school and a Sunday round. I hated the Sunday morning round because the papers were so heavy, as they all had magazine supplements. The morning round was the best because I could sneak a look at page three of *The Sun*, or the *Daily Sport*. After Monty retired, Neil Patel, who had a shop in the centre of town, took over the business, and I continued delivering papers.

I also worked on the local market on Tuesdays and Saturdays, helping to set up a flower stall before school and take it down after school.

When I was thirteen, I got a job at The Grove Hotel, collecting glasses in the over-25s singles bar that operated from a function room on Friday nights. I had to wear a white shirt and black trousers. The bar would be packed on a Friday night, and women would grab my backside all the time.

I was very much a kid of the 1980s. This was the era of bomber jackets, the first mobile phones and video games. I remember TV shows such as *Bullseye*, the darts game show, and the comedy programmes *Only Fools and Horses*, *Fawlty Towers* and *The Young Ones*. Tom and I were big fans of *Star Wars*, and we collected the plastic action figures.

I wasn't a massive music fan, but there was some great music in the 1980s, including Spandau Ballet, Michael Jackson, The Housemartins and Tina Turner. My favourite music was probably the soundtrack from *Rocky*.

What really dominated my childhood was football. I can remember watching England on TV in the 1986 World Cup in Mexico. That was when they lost 2–1 to Argentina in the quarter-final, going out to Maradona's Hand of God goal. Gary Lineker, who had left Leicester City the year before and signed for Everton, scored six goals in the tournament and won the Golden Boot award. I was so mad about football that if the England team brought out a record, I'd rush to Woolworths to buy it. I especially remember 'All the Way', which came out in 1988 to coincide with the European Championships in West Germany.

I would play football with some of my friends in the small park across the road from my house. We'd put our jumpers or coats down on the grass to make goals and play for hours. When I was nine, I joined Harborough Town Juniors, playing centre half, and I stayed with them until I was sixteen.

I started drinking and going to watch Leicester City play. When I was twelve, I went with some friends to Stoke to see Leicester play Port Vale. When my mum and dad asked me where I was going, I lied. I took the train to Leicester and then the football special train to Stoke. It was late when I arrived home after the match, which meant I'd missed taking part in the school swimming gala.

Another time, I went on the train to see Leicester play at Portsmouth. At Chichester, loads of Portsmouth fans got on and began jumping up and down in the carriage and chanting. One of them had the words 'skin up' tattooed on his arm. He asked me if I knew what it meant. Petrified, I shook my head. I thought he was going to beat me up, but he just laughed.

When I was thirteen, I bought a season ticket with the money I'd earned doing jobs. It cost forty pounds. I lived for Saturday afternoons. I'd either get the train to Leicester or take a Smiths coach that sometimes ran from Market Harborough to Filbert Street. I used to stand on the terrace in a corner of the ground called the Supporters' Club. I then changed to standing on The Kop, the noisiest area and the place where the Leicester troublemakers gathered. Leicester kept one of the pens empty unless there was a big demand for tickets. At one game, I remember Sheffield United fans throwing plastic cups of hot Bovril and coins at the Leicester fans.

My mum and dad took me to a few games. We travelled all over the country: to Brighton, only for the game to be called off; to Bournemouth, where we won 3–2 and it chucked it down during the match; and to Newcastle, where we got hammered 7–1. Leicester didn't have a great team until Martin O'Neill became manager in 1995 and won promotion to the Premier League at the end of his first season.

After my dad left Tungstone, he started his own screen-printing business in an industrial unit on a farm in Desborough, near Kettering. He printed mainly stickers, including a lot of Fat Willy stickers for surfboards, and he would drive all the way down to Cornwall to deliver them to shops there.

I'd go to the unit sometimes to help him. One of the jobs he gave me was to hang the printed material on a rack to dry. You had to do this carefully, making sure not to touch the wet paint. In some ways, I was a trainee screen printer. We'd take bags of rubbish to the back of the building and burn it all every week. Shortly before the England vs Brazil friendly at Wembley, for which I had a ticket, I was throwing rubbish onto what I thought was a dead fire when I noticed an aerosol can. I kicked it and it burst into flames. I remember screaming my head off. The pain where the flames had licked my face was unbearable, and my hair had been burned. My dad came running towards me. Bundling me into his car, he drove me straight to the A&E unit at Kettering General Hospital, which was about ten minutes away. I remember catching a glimpse of myself in the car's wing mirror and seeing skin hanging off my face. When we arrived at the hospital, I ran inside. The next thing I remember is waking up in the burns unit at Stoke Mandeville Hospital. I spent two weeks there. My hair was singed and I had blisters on my left hand where I'd held it up to shield my face.

The *Harborough Mail* ran a story about me on the front page with a photo. I had scars all over my face. The article mentioned that I was a Leicester fan and that I'd been due to go to Wembley to watch England play Brazil. A few days later, I was amazed to receive a football signed by all the members of the 1990 England World Cup squad as well as various items signed by Leicester City players, including Gary Mills, Paul Ramsey and Steve Walsh.

The *Evening Telegraph* also ran a story about me with the headline 'Brave James's Tragic Lesson'. It mentioned that a mother had asked me to talk to her two children, aged seven and ten, about the dangers of playing with matches.

When I returned to Welland Park, I was given a round of applause at the morning assembly to welcome me back. I had to wear sun cream for a long time. The doctors thought I might have to have skin grafts, but, thankfully, the scars eventually healed.

As a result of the publicity, two lads, Buzz and Tosh, who were seventeen, came up to me at the next Leicester game and said they recognised me from the photo in the paper. We became friends and I started going to the games and drinking with them. I'd buy cans of lager from an off-licence and we'd sit in the park drinking, or at the railway station. Sometimes we went to the Talbot, which vied with the Nags Head and the Red Cow for the distinction of being the roughest pub in the town. Bikers used to go there and some customers would stand around the bar openly smoking marijuana.

Often on Fridays we went to the Six Packs, which had a DJ. After last orders at eleven o'clock, there was a boogie bus every fifteen or twenty minutes that took people to the Broadway nightclub at the other end of the town. I was able to get in because one of the lads had given me a fake NUS card. If I was hungry on a Friday night, I'd head to Caspian's for one of their famous kebabs.

Given that I hadn't worked hard at school, I wasn't surprised by my GCSE results. I got a C in maths and English but failed everything else. Because I loved playing football for the school team, which was managed by Mr Bickley, the PE teacher, I stayed on and resat my GCSEs.

I didn't have a clear idea what I wanted to do after school, but I knew that I wanted to work in sport in some way, so I enrolled at Charles Keane College in Leicester to do a two-year BTec sports science course.

I couldn't believe it when the college arranged for me to have a trial at Leicester City. I went to the training ground at Belvoir Road and did quite well in the trial. I was over the moon when John Gregory, who was the number two to manager Brian Little and had played for Aston Villa, QPR and Derby County, told me I would be playing the following week in a match against Leicestershire Under-17s.

In the dressing room before the game, I made the mistake of calling John Gregory 'mate'. He jabbed me in the chest with his finger, yelling, 'You call me John.' I was shaken by his outburst. Of course, what he was doing was emphasising that the club had a strict code of discipline.

I played okay and we won 4–0. I felt I had a good chance of being signed by the club. One of the lads I played with was called Scott Eustace. He played one first-team game for Leicester but was then released. He went on to play for Mansfield Town, Chesterfield, Cambridge United and Lincoln City.

At the end of the game, the chief scout took me aside and told me I wasn't good enough to make it at Leicester City, but I might stand a chance with a team in one of the lower leagues. I duly wrote to a number of clubs in the third and fourth divisions asking if I could have a trial. Huddersfield Town, Lincoln City and Scunthorpe United wrote back and said they would be prepared to give me one. What I didn't mention was that I had a knee injury at the time. When I went along to Scunthorpe United, the coach could tell I had a problem with my knee. After the trial, he took me aside and said, 'What were you thinking, coming for a trial with a bad knee? Don't ever go to a trial with an injury again.'

I decided I wasn't going to ever make it as a professional footballer. Looking back, if I'm honest, I just wasn't good enough.

Things were getting tough at home. Dad's screen-printing company went out of business because some of his customers hadn't paid him, and our house in Cromwell Crescent was repossessed by the bank. The loan Dad had taken out had been secured against the house. I remember the father of one of my friends bringing his flat-back truck to help us move to a rented house on Welland Park Road.

I was seventeen and, with my hopes of becoming a professional footballer dashed, I still had no idea what I wanted to do with my life. But I knew I needed to start earning some money.

3

THE WORLD OF WORK

JUST AFTER I TURNED EIGHTEEN, I got a part-time job as a barman at the Grove Hotel. I enjoyed the work because of the fun atmosphere. As some of my friends often went there, it seemed more like a night out than work.

The Grove also made pizzas. When I wasn't working behind the bar, I'd deliver them in my battered white Ford Fiesta. I'd passed my driving test on my first attempt. My mum and dad had bought me driving lessons for my seventeenth birthday, and I only needed eleven of them before I took the test.

I applied for a job with KFC in Market Harborough and went to their branch in Kingsthorpe in Northampton for a week's training. I learned how to dip the chicken in the magic seasoning and drop it into the fryer, to make Zinger Burgers, and a lot about all the health and safety regulations that had to be complied with. I also got a free meal each day.

But I didn't take the job. I just couldn't face the ridicule I'd get in Market Harborough if people I knew saw me standing behind the counter in a KFC hat and uniform.

When the National Lottery was launched in 1994, I'd buy a ticket most weeks from Woolworths. One Saturday, I got four numbers correct. Based on the payouts from previous weeks, I reckoned that meant I'd won eighty pounds. I went straight out to work, but I also borrowed thirty quid from the manager of the Grove, telling him I'd pay him back when I collected my winnings on Monday morning. On Sunday evening, I went out with some of my mates to celebrate. However, when I went to Woolworths on Monday morning, it turned out there had been so many winners that I'd only won eighteen quid. I was gutted. I was now in debt to the manager.

One evening at the Grove, I found myself chatting to a girl called Charlotte. She was five years older than me and had a daughter who didn't live with her. I was later to discover that she'd been abused by her violent ex-partner, whom the police considered to be dangerous. Given what seemed a chaotic life, alarm bells should have rung. But if they did, I refused to hear them. Soon we were an item, and I was spending a lot of my time at her house. I don't ever remember going on a date with her. I just went to see her.

At the Grove one night, a customer called Mike said to me, 'Can you drive?'

'Yeah,' I replied.

'Do you want to earn some extra cash?'

'Doing what?'

'I need some potatoes delivered to some restaurants in Manchester.'

'What are you paying?'

'I'll give you a hundred quid.'

I hadn't driven much and I'd never driven anywhere as far as Manchester before, but, for that sort of money, I said I'd do it. Mike told me to meet him at a farm in Desborough at eight o'clock the next morning.

When I arrived, he was standing beside a green and red lorry piled high with bags of potatoes. I was speechless. I'd only ever driven a Fiesta; I didn't have a clue how to drive a lorry. With hindsight, of course, I should have said this to Mike. But I didn't.

'Here's the list of restaurants,' he said, handing me a sheet of paper. 'Shouldn't take you more than eight hours there and back.'

'Okay,' I murmured, hauling myself up into the cab.

I sat there looking at the unfamiliar controls, unsure of what to do. The steering wheel was much larger than the one in my car and I wasn't used to sitting this high up from the ground. I fiddled with the ignition key and the engine roared into action. I put my foot on the accelerator and gingerly moved off down the lane. *How on earth am I going to drive this all the way to Manchester and back?* When I reached the main road, I turned left, then immediately realised I'd gone the wrong way and should have turned right. I tried to reverse, but ended up on a grass verge, and the wheels became stuck in the mud. I desperately tried to get off the verge, but the lorry wouldn't move.

Mike appeared, looking angry. 'What the hell are you doing?' he shouted.

'It's stuck,' I said, getting out of the cab.

'How did you do that?'

'Dunno. It just happened.'

He climbed up into the cab and tried to move the lorry, but he couldn't.

'Look at what you've done!' he said, leaning out of the window.

'What?' I replied.

'You've burned out the bloody clutch!'

I don't remember precisely what he said after that, but I do remember that it wasn't complimentary.

Around this time I also did some work for a guy I knew who ran a building company. My job was to carry scaffolding poles, which was proper hard work. I'd be up at 5am and working on site from 7am to 5pm. I also had to dig foundations, which was just as hard. I realised then that I didn't want to end up doing that kind of work for the rest of my life. Today, when I look at people working on the roads in all weathers, I can't imagine how they do it.

My dad, or the father of one of my mates, occasionally hired a minibus to travel to away Leicester City games. We put Leicester banners on the windows and made V-signs at people in the street. We'd sing about striker Kevin Russell, who was bald, 'He's got no hair, but we don't care.' We thought it was great fun. But, of course, we were being idiots. We'd buy a twelve-pack and start drinking at eight in the morning and often stop at a pub along the way. We drank so much that often we wouldn't remember anything about the game. It was common back then to turn up at a game completely drunk and then try to make out you were sober to get into the ground.

Needless to say, we had a few incidents. One time, we went to see Leicester play Crystal Palace at Selhurst Park and got lost. We didn't get there until half-time, so we didn't bother going to see the game. On the way back, driving through central London, we were all singing and chanting and one of the group threw a beer can out of the window. When we stopped at the next traffic lights, a police van pulled up alongside us and several officers jumped out with their batons raised. They ordered us all out of the minibus and put us up against a wall. We were searched and had to give our names and addresses. They confiscated our beer, as a new law had come in that forbade the carrying of alcohol in vehicles going to sporting events. They gave us an escort all the way back up the M1 to Market Harborough, with one police car behind and one in front. Each time we entered a different county, local officers took over the escort. My dad tried to lose the police by turning off the motorway at the last second, but two police cars forced him to pull in. A police officer dragged him off the minibus and had him by the throat. A couple of lads who had got out and tried to run away were hit with batons. It all felt like a major overreaction. The only thing any of us had done was throw a beer can out of the window.

In 1994 we went to see Leicester play at Tranmere in the first leg of the play-off semi-final on a Sunday. And it was a disaster. To make a weekend of it, we decided to spend the night in Blackpool and travel down to Tranmere the next morning. My dad said he was going to stay in a hotel. The rest of us decided to sleep in the minibus. I ended up getting into a fight outside a nightclub, which left me with a massive black eye.

We set off down the M6 for Tranmere but we missed a turning and ended up somewhere in North Wales, where-upon we ran out of petrol. One of the lads eventually found some. The game ended 0–0. (Leicester beat Tranmere 2–1 in the second leg and then beat Derby County 2–1 in the final, winning promotion to the Premier League; Steve Walsh scored twice in the last few minutes.)

Heading back to Leicester on the M1, we got stuck in traffic. Some Derby fans on a coach spotted us. They jumped off and attacked us. The police came and we were all given a warning and told to go on our way.

Another time I went to Filbert Street with a friend in his car. As we got near the ground, the streets were thronged with Sheffield Wednesday fans. We gave them 'wanker' signs through the window. That was a big mistake because the car stalled and a load of angry Wednesday fans surrounded it and started rocking it and thumping on the windows. My friend and I were sitting there petrified, looking at all these angry faces staring in at us. We were only saved by the arrival of several police officers.

I never saw myself as a football hooligan. I just enjoyed taunting rival supporters. I didn't go looking for trouble. But I did seem to get caught up in it.

My relationship with Charlotte had soon become destructive. We were constantly arguing about something or other. One time, she kicked me incredibly hard on the leg because I wouldn't buy her cigarettes. If we had a bust-up, I'd go back to my mum and dad's and then a few days later I'd go back to Charlotte's. It was a vicious circle and it wasn't good for either of us. I should have realised that something wasn't quite right when she told me her daughter lived with her mum, whose house was around the corner.

I went out for a drink one night and said to Charlotte I'd be back before midnight. But I decided to go to the Broadway and didn't get back until two. I arrived at her flat to discover that the windows of my Fiesta had been smashed.

Charlotte was still up when I went inside.

'Did you smash the windows?' I asked, trying to stay calm.

'Yeah! And it serves you right,' she screamed.

'You're bloody nuts! Do you know how much it will cost to replace them?'

'That's your problem.'

It was futile arguing with her, so I just went to bed.

A few months after I first got together with Charlotte, she became pregnant. I was shocked. When I'd first met her, she'd told me she couldn't have any more children. I was only eighteen and the idea of becoming a father had never crossed my mind. Panic set in. I could see my life disappearing in front of me.

Charlotte gave birth to a baby girl on 15 September 1995 at Leicester General Hospital. I was by her side in the maternity ward when our daughter Hannah arrived. It was five o'clock in the morning, and I couldn't help feeling that this was how it was going to be from now on: up at the crack of dawn attending to the needs of a baby.

Charlotte and I were soon arguing again. She wanted to buy new baby items. I said we couldn't afford them, so we should buy second-hand ones. But she insisted on having everything brand new.

I dropped out of the course at Charles Keane College, partly because of my unexpected new role as a father, and partly because I wasn't committed enough to travel to and from Leicester each day. I just wanted to make money, especially as I now had a daughter to provide for. Some of my friends who hadn't gone to university had become apprentices. I'd thought about becoming an apprentice mechanic or something similar. I approached several companies who I thought might take me on, but they all said no.

I worked for a while at the Asda warehouse in Corby, putting orders on pallets and wrapping them in plastic, and I also worked at MRM in Market Harborough, packing Tampax in boxes. The more you packed in an hour, the more you got paid.

I ended up getting a job on the production line at the

Tungstone factory, following in my dad's footsteps. The company was one of the country's leading battery manufacturers and one of the biggest employers in the area. I didn't like the work, but the money was good and overtime was often available. Sometimes I'd get told off for being too quick, and sometimes I'd get told off for being too slow. Before the end of the shift, everyone had to have a shower because of all the lead in the air, and we were tested regularly for lead poisoning. If the level was too high, you'd be sent to work in the warehouse for a while. I couldn't imagine staying more than 10 years at Tungstone, as my dad had done.

I started playing football each week with some of my mates in the sports hall at the leisure centre. Because Buzz worked there as a lifeguard and gym instructor, we were allowed to use the hall at 10pm. Sometimes we'd still be playing at nearly midnight, and I'd have to be at Tungstone's at 6am to begin my shift. Eventually, I formed a six-aside team, Real Lions, and we joined the six-aside league on Monday evenings at Welland Park College.

Fed up with working at Tungstone's, I applied for a job as a trainee carpet fitter with H. Monk & Sons, a home-furnishings shop on Northampton Road that had first opened in 1895. When I went for the interview, I was told I'd be paid £70 per week, but could earn £200 a week once I was fully qualified.

I went out in the van with Gary, the head fitter. He'd pick me up just before nine and we'd go to the shop and collect the carpets. We usually did two or three jobs a day. We always did the minimum and often took a two-hour lunch break. You'd go to some houses and the people wouldn't have moved all the furniture from a room, or the old carpet would still be down. You'd have to move the furniture and take up the old carpet. The best houses were new-builds, where you just whacked the carpet down. I made lots of mistakes when I first started, such as cutting the carpet too close to the skirting board or cutting it too short. To stretch a carpet, you had to put a pad on it and then knee it into the skirting board. This wasn't easy.

After about eighteen months of this, I felt restless. I needed a change. My life felt aimless and I felt trapped in my relationship with Charlotte. There had to be a life beyond the streets of Market Harborough.

Peter Frisby, known as Friz, one of my closest friends, had joined the Royal Navy after leaving school. When he came home on leave, we'd meet up in the Nags Head or the Red Cow for a drink, and he'd tell me he was having the time of his life. He'd sailed all over the world and visited loads of countries. I began to think that maybe the Navy was for me too. I was young, fit and healthy and although I hadn't done well at school, I considered myself reasonably bright. What's more, if I joined up, I'd be away from the destructive cycle of my relationship with Charlotte.

One morning, I took a train to Leicester and made my way to the Armed Forces Careers Office. I walked in and said to a guy in a blue-grey uniform behind a desk that I was interested in joining the Royal Navy. He looked me up and down and told me to take a seat. He then asked me various questions about my life and why I was interested in the Navy.

'Have you thought about the RAF?' he asked.

I shook my head. 'I don't know anything about it.'

'I'm in the RAF.'

'Oh.'

'It's a great career.'

'But I don't know about planes and flying and all that kind of stuff.'

'You don't have to. You could train to be an aircraft

technician, a chef, a nurse or lots of other things. There's so many opportunities.'

I took his advice and decided to apply, even though I had no interest in aircraft. I didn't have a clue what kind of career I wanted in the RAF. And I probably didn't care what I did. My grandad had been in the RAF, but that hadn't ever meant anything to me. He never spoke about it. He was generally too busy talking about Leicester City.

Not long after this visit to the careers office, I was invited back there to take a test to see what type of jobs I might be suitable for in the RAF. I thought I'd like to be a physical trainer. Unfortunately so did many others who were looking to join. Instead, I was offered a job as a supplier, which, I was told, might involve refuelling, looking after electronics, working in the warehouse or receiving and dispatching. In fact, I ended up doing a lot of office work.

I had developed a bad knee due to all the football I was playing, and it was causing me a lot of pain. When I went to see my GP about it, he said I should see a consultant, but it could take up to a year just to get an appointment. So I took out a loan of £2,000 to go private. I managed to see a consultant, have a scan, get the results and then have an operation to trim the cartilage, all in less than a week.

When I received a letter inviting me to join the RAF, I accepted it, signing a nine-year contract, but I never mentioned my bad knee. The day before I joined, I had to go back to the recruitment office in Leicester to sign all the papers and swear allegiance to the Queen. I had mixed emotions about joining up. It was a way out of my relationship with Charlotte, and it could provide me with a career. On the other hand, I would see a lot less of my daughter, and I still wasn't sure the military was for me. What would happen if I couldn't adapt to life in the

RAF? How tough would it be? I had signed up for nine years. Would I be able to leave?

Whatever was to happen, I was about to embark on a very different life to the one I'd been used to.

4

MY MILITARY CAREER

THE NEXT DAY, MY DAD DROVE ME to RAF Halton, near Aylesbury in Buckinghamshire, where I would be doing my basic training. After I signed in, I was given an introduction pack, bedding, my uniform and two boiler suits. The rule was that, for your first seventeen days, you wore one of these suits. After that, you would wear your uniform. I was then directed to a room where a barber was waiting behind a chair. All new recruits had to have short haircuts.

The base consisted of a number of red-brick accommodation blocks and other buildings that variously housed administration offices, a hospital, a sports centre and stores. RAF Halton was primarily a base for providing training. I'd expected to see fighter planes lined up on the airfield. Instead, all I saw were a couple of gliders.

That evening, all the new recruits assembled in a lecture theatre, and a sergeant major gave us an introduction to life on the base and the basic training course. He warned, 'Not all of you will make it. The training is designed to make or break you.' I sat there wondering what I had let myself in for.

I slept in a dormitory with about twenty other guys. We had to clean it each day so that it was spotless. Sometimes you could be cleaning until midnight.

Most of the other recruits were around the same age as me, and they were from all over the country. Talking to some of them, I discovered that joining the RAF had been their dream. Many had been in the cadets. That made them very different from me, with my complete lack of affinity with the RAF.

The eight weeks of basic training turned out to be the hardest thing I've ever done. An alarm woke us at 5.30am and we had to quickly put on our uniforms, make our beds in a particular way, go to breakfast and wait for the inspection at 7.30am. If you hadn't made your bed correctly, you'd have to make it again. Your uniform and your shoes would also be inspected. Because I felt so much pressure to pass, I'd get my bed ready and then sleep on the floor because I didn't want to mess it up and have to make it again in the morning.

The training and regime were sheer mental torture and you got little sleep. Some days, I wondered how on earth I was going to continue. We had to march across the parade ground every morning wearing heavy backpacks and then do drills. The commanding officers would shout at us. You couldn't answer back. You just had to stand there and take it. What we were being taught was discipline.

You weren't allowed to watch TV or listen to the radio, but you could make phone calls. And you weren't allowed to walk around the base; you had to march everywhere, even if you were on your own.

From day one, the RAF tries to break you. I was pushed to

the limit both physically and mentally. My knee, which was still recovering from the operation, gave me a lot of pain during drill: stamping my leg down and performing about-turns really made the pain flare up. But I couldn't tell anyone about it, because I'd have to reveal I'd had the operation. I had to just carry on through it, not least because I needed to earn enough money to pay off the loan for the procedure.

There was a good camaraderie among the recruits. We all helped each other out. When I struggled to fasten my tie with a Windsor knot, one of the other lads showed me how to do it. Each day there were competitions between different flights, which was what the RAF called groups of recruits. The winners were allowed to listen to the radio; I remember listening to an England game one night. If you passed the inspection on day seventeen, you were allowed home for the weekend.

Each week, we did different types of training, such as weapons, first aid or chemical and biological warfare. Part of the chemical and biological warfare training involved going into a chamber in which tear gas was then released. You were told not to rub your eyes. Afterwards, I stumbled out coughing, my eyes stinging. Some of the other recruits were throwing up. Staff were on hand to rinse our eyes with water.

On Fridays we took a test to see what we'd learned from the training. If you failed, you had to resit the test on the Sunday and remain at the base for the weekend. If you failed again, you had to repeat the entire week's training. I managed to pass the training with just one failure, in weapons. Picking up a gun for the first time felt strange. Being on the firing range and firing live rounds was scary.

We did drill most days in preparation for the passing-out period at the end of the eight weeks' training. We marched holding rifles with bayonets attached. If you didn't look straight ahead, the commanding officer would march over to you and scream in your face.

Eventually, this gruelling period came to an end. Charlotte and my mum and dad came to my passing-out parade. My parents had now split up. Their marriage had been under a strain ever since my dad lost his business and the house. I felt sad for both of them. I'd had a happy childhood and they had done their best for me and for Tom and Debbie. They had now given up the house in Welland Park Road; my mum had moved into a flat near the river, and my dad rented a house.

I felt incredibly proud as I marched across the parade ground, swinging my arms while the band played. We had to obey commands such as 'Present arms', 'Change arms', 'About turn', which all had to be done in time. After the parade, there was a buffet and drinks for everyone. Passing out was a huge achievement for me. Tough as the experience had been, I'd made it, but others hadn't.

The RAF taught you discipline and gave you a structure. Before joining, I didn't have much of this in my life. I now had a focus and a sense of purpose.

I was informed I'd be staying on at RAF Halton for a further eight weeks to train to work in supply. Thankfully, this turned out to be much more chilled-out than the basic training, but the relaxed atmosphere had its downsides. One Wednesday evening, after a few drinks, I got into a fight in the bar with one of the other lads. We'd been watching Leicester play Middlesbrough in the Carling Cup Final replay. I'd been to Wembley on the Sunday to watch the first leg, which ended 1–1. The fight happened after a silly argument over something, and this lad ended up sitting on top of me. I was arrested by the military police and chucked into a cell. The next morning, they marched me into breakfast to make an example of me.

Afterwards, they marched me back to the cell. My only consolation was that Leicester won the replay 1–0, thanks to a Steve Claridge goal after extra time.

I had to attend a disciplinary hearing, and I was put on jankers for three days, which meant I wasn't allowed off base. I had to report to the guard room before breakfast in the morning and do menial jobs, such as painting lines on the parade ground or cleaning, in what should have been my free time.

I was then posted to RAF Cottesmore in Rutland, which was home to the Tri-National Tornado Training Establishment. Panavia Tornado aircrews from the RAF, German Air Force, German Navy air arm and the Italian Air Force all trained there.

My relationship with Charlotte continued to be volatile. One time while I was home on leave, I met a friend for a drink to celebrate his birthday. Someone in the pub offered me a ticket for the Leicester game that night, and I decided to go. I phoned Charlotte to tell her. She wasn't happy. 'If you go to the game, I'll have burned all your clothes by the time you get back,' she said. I didn't take this threat seriously. But when I got back to her house later that night, there was a smouldering pile of ashes on the front lawn. Needless to say, we ended up in another argument.

Charlotte would regularly put Hannah in a car seat and dump her at my mum's front door, saying, 'Here, you have her.' She would also often phone the police, alleging I'd hit her, and three cars would turn up. This became a regular occurrence. The police got fed up with being called out so often, and we both ended up in court and were bound over to keep the peace.

The only time I can remember the relationship being good was when we went on holiday to the Costa Brava in the summer of 1997, when Hannah was two. We travelled by coach all the way from Leicester. I learned that trying to keep a two-year-old entertained on a twenty-four-hour journey wasn't easy. On a couple of occasions, Hannah crawled under the seat and fell asleep.

We stayed on a large camp site about a mile from the sea. One day, I couldn't find Hannah and began to panic. I ran to the swimming pool, where I found her happily sitting beside the water slide.

That holiday sticks in my mind for another reason. On the last day, we were waiting for the coach to take us back to Leicester when someone shouted out that Princess Diana was dead. I didn't believe it at first. Realising it was true, I felt stunned. The most famous woman in the world had been killed in a car crash in an underpass in Paris. It didn't seem real.

I knew I'd be posted overseas soon, and there was a rumour on the base that it would be Kosovo, where British soldiers had been deployed on a peace-keeping mission. I thought being in a conflict zone would be exciting. I might end up helping to refuel planes or helicopters. But when the announcement was made, I discovered that I'd be going to the Falklands.

Just before Christmas in 2000, along with about fifty other guys, I was taken by coach to RAF Brize Norton in Oxfordshire, where we boarded a Hercules. We strapped ourselves in and prepared for the long flight. I'd met a few guys who had been posted to the Falklands who said the place was dull and cold with nothing much to do. Trying to stay positive, I told myself that being stationed on a remote island might turn out to be an adventure.

Fifteen hours later, after stopping at Ascension Island to refuel, we landed at RAF Mount Pleasant, about thirty miles from Stanley, the capital of the Falklands. It was pouring with rain and a wind was whipping up from the Atlantic. Mount Pleasant was divided up between the RAF and the Army. The base had a gym, cinema, bowling alley, Olympic-size swimming pool and other facilities to help military personnel deal with living in such a remote place. I remember seeing Gurkhas proudly marching around.

I shared a room with another guy and was given a job in an office, dealing with accounts and orders. To earn extra money, I worked in a bar and a café.

There was a big drinking culture at the base. In your free time, you either trained or you drank. I tried to train hard in the week, but on Friday and Saturday nights I'd just get smashed. Being on the Falklands was a bit like being in a pressure cooker – you felt cut off from everywhere – and sometimes I got so drunk, I'd wake up in all sorts of places. One of my senior officers told me I should stop drinking, which was probably good advice.

I played football on Wednesday afternoons and went to the gym when I could. I used to train with a flight-lieutenant, and we became good friends. Another officer, seeing us together, assumed I must be an officer too, and I didn't put him right, even when he invited me for a drink in the officers' mess. For other ranks to enter that space is one of the worst things you can do in the military. Unsurprisingly, I was quickly spotted. I got a serious ticking-off.

I volunteered to be a spotter on a plane that flew around the Falklands searching for illegal fishing boats. It would fly quite low in order to get a good look at anyone fishing. If an illegal vessel was spotted, the Royal Navy would be informed and would send a ship to intercept it. On one occasion, some Argentinian Special Forces kit was seen on a boat with no one on it. I never discovered what the story was.

The Falklands is a British overseas territory, which means its skies are UK airspace. If an unauthorised plane entered that airspace, sirens would sound on the base and Tornado jets would be scrambled. They would be in the air within six minutes.

A sergeant arranged a weekend at an RAF refuelling post beside a lake. I was taken with a small group of guys in a Chinook and dropped off at the top of a mountain. Before we boarded the Chinook, we were told to put our jackets on, but I didn't listen, as it was warm. We trekked to the bottom in freezing conditions and pouring rain, and I got absolutely drenched, which taught me a lesson. We spent several days at the refuelling post, which was a welcome break from the base. I went fishing in a boat on the lake for salmon, which we cooked on the barbecue in the evening.

I also went to Sea Lion Island, where there were sea lions and penguins, and there was an option to go to Ascension Island, in the middle of the Atlantic just south of the equator, for four days rest and relaxation. After the cold and wet of the Falklands, I really fancied lying on a beach in the sun for my four days, which I thought I'd take on my way home from the Falklands, when my time there came to an end. To qualify for R&R on Ascension, you had to have served in the Falklands before. To get around this, I asked a mate who worked in the office where they stamped the service cards to give mine an extra stamp. Other people had got away with this, but I was caught out. My commanding officer was not happy and I spent my last four days on the islands, in what should have been my precious R&R time, confined to barracks.

Being in the Falklands had been an interesting experience, but there really hadn't been a lot to do. My next posting – at RAF Cottesmore, about twenty-five miles from Market

Harborough – came as a great relief.

The RAF gave me an opportunity to learn to ski in the mountains of Colorado. It was seen as a team-building exercise. About fifty of us went, flying British Airways from Heathrow. We stayed in condominiums in Aspen and other resorts. I'd never been on skis before, but I loved it. There were six groups, with group one for the most experienced skiers and group six for those who had never skied. I started off in the novice group, but by day ten I'd moved into group two.

Otherwise, if I had a few days off, I would sometimes go to Magaluf in Majorca to see my brother Tom. The arrival of budget airlines, such as EasyJet and Ryanair, meant the flights were really cheap.

Tom worked in a bar called Poco Loco, which claimed to be the best disco-party pub in Magaluf. Inside there were two large bars and a resident British DJ playing hits from the sixties to the nineties. Club 18–30 would put on bar crawls and the Poco Loco was always a key stopping-point. Most of the tourists were Brits, but there were quite a few Scandinavians and Germans too. As all the bar staff knew I was Tom's brother, I never had to pay for drinks. I'd drink on my own when I was waiting for Tom to finish his shift, which, I discovered, was a great way to meet members of the opposite sex.

After Tom finished work, we'd go to the bars along what was known as 'the Strip'. Two of the liveliest places were Boomerangs and Underground, where everyone did stupid dances. Sometimes we'd end up sleeping on the beach.

One time, Tom and I got kicked out of his flat in the middle of the night, as he hadn't told his landlord I was staying there. We had to sleep on the street. On another occasion, I fell asleep in an amusement arcade and woke up to find my wallet and shoes had been stolen.

That was a minor concern compared to an incident that happened on a night out closer to home. When I was on leave in Market Harborough, I'd try to go to see Leicester City play if they were at home. After one game, I went out for a drink with Buzz, Stevie and some other mates, and then we went to the Broadway. As it was always difficult to get a taxi from the club, we decided to walk home. Near the train station, Buzz got into a fight with a lad called Nino, who was from Northampton and with another group of lads. Nino was in a wheelbarrow that had been stolen from a builders' merchant. It turned into a real brawl, and Nino ended up with a broken leg.

A couple of weeks later, I received a phone call from the police asking me to attend Market Harborough police station. When I was interviewed, I told them I'd tried to break up the fight, but the officer interviewing me said several witnesses had claimed they'd seen someone fitting my description either kick Nino or stamp on his head. I was arrested and charged with actual bodily harm. Buzz and Stevie were also arrested.

The three of us appeared at Market Harborough Magistrates' Court and pleaded not guilty. We were told we would be tried at crown court. I phoned my sergeant at the RAF base to explain what had happened. He wasn't happy, and informed me that when the trial took place, an RAF officer would have to attend.

It was a year before we went on trial, at Leicester Crown Court. On the first day, all the witnesses said that I'd been responsible for Nino's broken leg, but that was ridiculous – I was just trying to break up the fight. Fortunately, there were lots of inconsistencies in their accounts. It also emerged that Nino had previous convictions for a number of offences, including violence. I was surprised that this information was given.

I left the court feeling worried, and in tears. I was sure that

I'd be found guilty.

On the morning of the second day, the judge instructed the jury to find Stevie not guilty, and he walked away free. He had always maintained he hadn't done anything, and so had Buzz initially, but by this time he had shifted to a self-defence plea.

When the pair of us gave evidence, we were both cross-examined at length. My barrister talked about my career in the RAF and said that I had a young daughter.

The jury was sent out to deliberate, returning after a couple of hours or so.

Buzz was told to stand up first.

'How do you find the defendant Mark Burrows?' said the judge.

'Not guilty,' said the foreman.

Then it was my turn to get to my feet.

'How do you find James Longley?'

By this point I was quaking. I reckoned the jury was bound to find one out of three of us guilty. With Stevie and Buzz walking free, that one person was going to be me. I had a clear vision of ending up in prison.

When the foreman said 'not guilty', the wave of relief that surged through me was extraordinary. It was honestly one of the best feelings I have ever had in my life, before or since.

I had now finally split from Charlotte. The relationship was always doomed to fail, as we just weren't right for each other, and it shouldn't have lasted as long as it did. With hindsight, I don't think I handled the relationship very well and I have to share the blame for what happened. Charlotte had now left Leicestershire and moved to Devon with Hannah. I was saddened that she was gone and I wouldn't be able to see her, but I had no choice but to crack on with life. At that time, unmarried fathers had no legal right to see their children. I had no more idea where she was than if she'd been kidnapped.

The RAF had a boat and a caravan at Tallington Lakes, near Stamford, and I used to go there some weekends. We'd water-ski, then have a barbecue and a few drinks in the evening. That led to my taking part in the RAF Water Ski Championships at the National Water Sports Centre in Nottingham. After the competition, I met a girl at a bar and she invited me back to her place, where I spent the night. I was woken the following morning by someone hammering on the front door. I was naked and on the sofa in the living room. The girl hurried downstairs with a duvet wrapped around her.

'Shit!' she muttered under her breath.

'What's up?' I asked.

'It's my bloody boyfriend.'

'Bloody hell!' I could see trouble here.

'Say you're John's mate!'

'John?'

'Yeah, just say it.'

A big angry-looking guy stomped in.

'And who the fuck are you?' he demanded.

'I'm John's mate,' I said, not knowing who John was.

'John's mate?'

'Yeah.'

As he followed the girl upstairs, I got dressed as quickly as I could, but I could only find one sock.

'Run!' the girl yelled.

I left and sprinted down the street. I knew I was in Nottingham, but I didn't have a clue whereabouts. Seeing a bus, I jumped on it. I looked out of the back window and saw that the guy was following the bus in a car, and there was another guy sitting beside him. I was in big trouble, and I needed to think of a way out. I asked a lady if I could borrow her mobile phone to call the police. She handed it to me, and within a couple of minutes a squad car arrived. I explained what had happened, and, after a brief interview at the police station, they took me back to the water sports centre.

I was on an easy number in the RAF, but I didn't like the job. I'd do ten days on and eleven days off, or four on, four off. You did days and nights. If your days fell on a weekend, you were just on call. If you were on nights, you started at eight. The shift patterns kept changing.

A lorry used to turn up with kit at one in the morning, and you'd unload it. Some nights there wasn't much on it, and you'd be finished by two, so you could sleep until seven when the place opened up. I kept a mattress and sleeping bag in my locker, although I wasn't meant to.

I retook my maths and English GCSEs and did a business studies course. I asked about becoming an officer, getting promotion or changing job. I was told promotion wasn't an option, as I'd been in trouble several times. Each occasion, of course, was alcohol-related.

After one year in the RAF, you became a senior aircraftsman. There were blokes there who were still senior aircraftsmen after sixteen years; they were never going to get promoted. They would stay in for twenty-two years and leave with a pension. I didn't want to be like that.

The money wasn't great in the RAF: I was on about sixteen grand. Tax and NI came out of this and also food and accommodation. So I applied to Harborough District Council for a licence to drive a taxi. On my days off and at weekends, I began driving for a guy called John Marlow in his six-seater Renault Espace. Johnny had a tragic claim to fame in the area:

his son Danny had been murdered by a hitman in 1997 over a forty-pound debt relating to a snooker game. I had known Danny because he used to drive around Market Harborough selling videos, including pirate copies, from the back of a van.

When I was driving, I'd have Johnny's phone, but it was rare that someone phoned for a taxi. I picked up most of the customers at the rank in the high street or outside the railway station. I established a good reputation, and people would phone me because I'd never refuse a job. It was good fun driving the taxis, especially at night when most customers were drunk. It was almost a social thing. There was always the odd fare who looked like they might throw up or was hard to wake when they got home, but more often than not it was good fun.

You meet all sorts of people as a taxi driver. I had passengers who had fallen asleep on trains and ended up in Market Harborough when they should have got off in Loughborough or Kettering. They'd emerge uncertainly from the station, looking around, and then spot my car and ask me to take them home.

I came close to being assaulted on several occasions. I was especially wary of taking travellers anywhere. While some were fine, others had a reputation for not paying. One time, I picked up a couple of guys with Irish accents, whom I took to be travellers, in Leicester and they asked to go to Loughborough. When I said that was too far, one of them, who was holding a bottle, threatened me. I politely explained that I didn't have the time to drive all the way to Loughborough and back. After some arguing, to my relief, they eventually got out of the car.

I've chased people for non-payment. I once rugby-tackled a guy in Kibworth. Another time, I took a girl home at half-three in the morning. When I reached her home, she said she had to go in to get the money to pay me. After several minutes she hadn't appeared, so I thought she had done a runner. I wasn't sure which house she had gone into, but then I saw her footprints in the fresh snow, so I followed them. I knocked on the door and she opened up. She said she didn't have enough money to pay me, but she would give me some jewellery instead. I wasn't happy with the arrangement, but I took the jewellery. I gave her my phone number and said when she had the money to pay me, she could have it back. A few days later she came to the cab office and paid, and I returned her jewellery.

In 2001 I applied for a place on a business information systems degree course at University College Northampton as a mature student. I told the university that I was still in the RAF and might have to miss the odd lecture. I swapped shifts at the base when I could. So my life now was at full throttle: I was doing shifts in the RAF, driving taxis at night, not getting much sleep, and then driving to lectures.

I also had a relationship with my daughter to maintain. Even though Hannah was now living with Charlotte in Barnstaple, I still managed to see her – if Charlotte allowed me to. I'd finish driving the taxi at 3am and then drive to Bristol, which was the halfway point, and stop for a rest. Sometimes I'd pull over before Bristol, as I couldn't keep my eyes open. I'd sleep in the car for a few hours and then continue the journey.

Charlotte wouldn't let me pick Hannah up and take her out. I could only see her for two hours at a contact centre. Being observed by members of staff as I watched Hannah paint or read her a story didn't seem natural. What I wanted to do was take her to the park or out somewhere, but it was better than nothing. It would be around eight o'clock by the time I arrived back in Market Harborough. After grabbing something to eat,

I'd go out in the taxi and work until five or six in the morning.

On one occasion, I phoned the contact centre to say that, because of the traffic, I was going to be twenty minutes late. I hadn't realised it was the school holidays. When I arrived, Hannah wasn't there; her granny had taken her home. One of the members of staff at the centre had explained to her that I'd be late, but she refused to wait.

To prevent me from seeing Hannah, Charlotte and her mum made false allegations about my dad and me. My contact with my daughter was stopped and I had to see a solicitor and go to court to get it reinstated. Charlotte would phone out of the blue and leave voicemail messages for me, but I ignored them, as there was no point in talking to her. She never listened and would just shout at me down the phone. Hannah was eventually taken into care for several months – even then I wasn't told – and then went to live with her granny.

I didn't have a good relationship with Charlotte's mother. I didn't like her and she didn't like me. But I can see now that she was trying to protect her daughter, and there's no doubt that she made a good job of bringing up Hannah, who has grown up to become an amazing person considering the upheaval she want through as a child.

I didn't feel I should have to pay any money to Charlotte if she wasn't going to let me see Hannah. Charlotte contacted the Child Support Agency (CSA), and they wrote to me and asked me to complete a form with information about my income and my overheads. I did this, and shortly afterwards I received a letter saying I would have to pay around £350 per month. This was a huge amount. I was still paying off the loan for my knee operation at the private hospital and I had credit-card debts. Once I'd paid the CSA, I was left with more or less nothing.

That lack of money was one of the reasons I decided to leave the RAF. Equally, I couldn't really see my career progressing because of my misdemeanours. It was a big decision, but an easy one. Comfortable as it could be, I'd never felt I fitted into RAF life. I enjoyed the sports side of things, but that was about it.

I had to give twelve months' notice. I had built up six or eight weeks' leave and a thirty-days resettlement, so this was deducted. During the last few months, I was rarely at the base. Although I had a room there, I didn't sleep in it very often.

To mark the end of my RAF career, I invited some of the guys for a drink at the Thursday disco in the NAAFI. It turned out to be a memorable night, but for the wrong reasons. At some point during the evening, I fell over on the dance floor and injured my left arm. When I woke up in the morning, I was in great pain. I drove myself to hospital, which wasn't easy with the use of only one hand. When a doctor examined me, she told me I'd ruptured a joint in my shoulder. It was an injury more common in rugby players than dance-floor casualties, she said.

With my time in the RAF over, I wanted to be close to the university so I rented a freezing basement room in a house in Northampton with five female students. After a few months, however, I returned to Market Harborough and moved into a rented flat above the Oxfam shop with Buzz. My bedroom was the same height as the clock tower – and the clock chimed every hour. Buzz and I furnished the flat with stuff we picked up at the local tip. The flat was in a great location, just two doors away from the Talbot, where Buzz and I often drank. At closing time, we'd invite friends back for a party.

I continued taxi-driving, but money remained tight. I'd heard from someone that a guy who ran a shop in the town was selling fake twenty-pound notes for seven quid each. This sounded like a good deal, so I bought a load of them. I would use them at the Talbot to pay for all my drinks.

What I was doing was illegal, of course. If I thought I'd get away with it, I was wrong.

5

'HE WOULDN'T TAKE ME HOME'

IT STARTED OFF AS A NIGHT OUT with Buzz and a few other mates, but it ended with an incident that was to turn my life upside down – sending me into the depths of despair, but also putting me on the road to becoming a multi-millionaire.

On a warm evening in August 2002, I had caught the train to Leicester for the stag do of my friend Max, whom I had known since school. We were both twenty-six. I was pleased that Max had met someone he wanted to settle down with. In my case, I didn't feel ready to spend my life with just one person. Or maybe it was because I hadn't met the right person. I'd only left the RAF a few months earlier, and I was still adapting to being back in civvy street.

But life was pretty good: I was allowed to see my seven-year-old daughter, I was making reasonable money from driving taxis and I was revising for my first-year exams for my degree in business systems and information.

Our spirits were high when we went into a busy pub in the city centre for the first drink of the night. And we knew it was going to be a long night. We had a couple more drinks, ribbing Max about getting married in the way that blokes do.

'That's it now, mate,' said Steve. 'You'll be under the thumb.'

Max waved him away playfully.

'Yeah, no more going to the pub with us lot,' said Buzz.

We left the pub and made our way to the Jongleurs comedy club in Granby Street, which had a great reputation for a fun night out. After we'd bought our drinks at the bar, we found an empty table and sat down to wait for the first act. I can't remember who the comedian was, but some of our group startled heckling him. This didn't go down well, and one of the bouncers came over and told us to tone it down. But Buzz continued to heckle. The bouncer told him if he carried on, we'd all be thrown out. I got up to go to the toilet, which meant navigating my way through the crowded venue. When I returned to the table, my mates had all disappeared. Thinking they might be at the bar, I did my best to search the busy venue, but they were nowhere to be seen. So I drank up and left.

I headed to a nearby pub that my mates sometimes went to, but there was no sign of them. I stayed for a pint anyway, then decided to go to Krystals nightclub in Church Gate, somewhere they all went to occasionally. Krystals was heaving. I wandered around but couldn't see any of them. *Now I'm here*, I thought, *I might as well stay for a while and enjoy the music.* The DJ was pumping out hits such as 'How You Remind Me' by Nickelback, 'Work It' by Missy Elliott and 'Long Time Gone' by the Dixie Chicks. I downed a few more drinks, feeling chilled and at peace with the world.

I left Krystals at about two in the morning. I'd stayed much longer than I'd planned and was a bit the worse for wear. I was also starving. I saw the lights of a takeaway in the distance and, unsteadily, made my way along the street towards it. After buying fried chicken and chips and a can of Coke, I went to find a taxi to take me home to Market Harborough. Despite the lateness of the hour, there were still plenty of people out. And, inevitably, like me, many were virtually legless. I crossed the road to avoid a fight that had broken out between two groups of guys. A girl in a short skirt was screaming her head off and trying to pull one of the guys away. I could hear police sirens getting closer.

Eventually, I found a taxi near the clock tower and asked the driver to take me to Market Harborough, which was about a twenty-five-minute drive.

'Yeah, okay,' he said, speaking through the window.

'Cheers.'

'You have to pay up front.'

'How much?'

'Twenty-five quid.'

'Okay, mate,' I said. 'Let me go to the cashpoint.' Being a taxi driver myself, I understood why he was asking for the money in advance. I'd had my fair share of late-night customers who had legged it without paying when I dropped them off.

I wove my way across the road to a cashpoint, throwing my takeaway carton into a bin, and withdrew the money for the taxi. I got into the front seat and gave the driver my address, taking a sip of my Coke as he moved off. We passed the deserted railway station and were soon heading south along London Road and out of the city. As the taxi sped along the B6047, my eyelids began to droop. I held on to my can of Coke, occasionally taking a sip to help me stay awake. When we passed McDonald's and the BP garage and drove up the hill towards Gartree prison, I knew we weren't far from Market

Harborough.

What I remember next is waking up and discovering the taxi had stopped. I looked around anxiously. It was pitch black.

'What's going on?' I said to the driver, peering into the darkness.

'I want more money!' he demanded.

'What for?'

'Look,' he said, pointing at the seat. 'You've spilt your drink.'

I glanced down. The Coke can was lying in the footwell, and his seat and one of his trouser legs were wet.

'It was an accident.'

'You pay extra!'

'I haven't got any more money.'

Then I realised he was holding my wallet in his hand. I snatched it from him.

'You have to pay for this!'

'Listen, mate, I've told you I've no more money.'

'I'm taking you back to Leicester then.'

'You're bloody well not. You're taking me home.'

'If you don't pay, I'm taking you to the police station in Leicester.'

'No way! You're taking me to Harborough.'

He put the key in the ignition and started to turn the car around. I grabbed hold of the steering wheel.

'You're taking me home!' I shouted at him.

'You give me more money!' he said, trying to wrench the steering wheel from me. We grappled with it. When he tried to shove me away, I pulled my fist back and punched him in the face, knocking him towards the window. I hit him again. He tried to grab me around the throat, so I landed another punch.

At that moment another taxi appeared. I saw that it was being driven by a bloke I knew, and his passenger was Guy, who ran the Talbot, and for whom my mum had been a child-minder when I was a kid. He and the two blokes he was with leapt out of their car, yanked open the passenger door of the taxi I was in and pulled me out.

'James! What do you think you're doing?' screamed Guy.

'He wouldn't take me home,' I said.

Guy ordered me to get in his taxi, which I did. He and the driver then took me home.

I woke up the following morning feeling rough. It was nearly ten o'clock. I lay there, replaying what had happened a few hours earlier: Krystals, going to the cashpoint, getting into a taxi by the clock tower, the BP garage, seeing the Coke can in the foot well, grabbing my wallet, trying to grapple the steering wheel from the driver, punching him. What had I done? Would the taxi driver go to the police? Would he say I'd attacked him? These and other questions raced through my mind.

I expected a knock on the door, but nothing happened. As the days went by, my anxiety subsided. The taxi driver probably hadn't reported the incident. Perhaps he was here illegally. I'd had a close shave, I told myself, and I resolved never to get into a situation like that again. I wouldn't have hit the guy if he'd taken me home. But I still felt he'd provoked me: he tried to turn the car round and take me back to Leicester.

Then one morning at around seven o'clock, there was a loud knock on the door of the house where I was staying, which belonged to my girlfriend at the time, Lucy. I went downstairs and opened it. Four police officers were standing there.

'James Longley?' said one of them.

'Yeah.'

'I'm arresting you on suspicion of actual bodily harm.'

'What?'

'Come with us, please.'

I was led into a waiting police van and told I was being taken to Wigston Police Station. On the way, however, the van stopped at Market Harborough Police Station. There the back doors were opened and a CID officer I knew from the gym was looking in at me.

'Hello James,' he said. 'We've also had an allegation concerning fake currency, and we've got a warrant to search your address. Before we start, is there anything we might find?'

If the day had started badly, it was now turning into a catastrophe. Arrested for one offence before breakfast, I was learning ten minutes later that I was in trouble over a completely different offence. My heart raced as I tried to work out what to say. I knew I had seventeen fake twenty-pound notes in my car, but there was nothing in the house.

'No,' I said, truthfully.

Almost immediately afterwards, I regretted saying that. They would trash the house anyway, and it wasn't even my house, so I was effectively inflicting a horrible experience on Lucy, who was totally blameless. But when you're under that kind of enormous pressure, what do you do?

Arriving at Wigston, I was booked in and taken to a cell. The duty solicitor came to see me and explained what was going to happen next. He said I didn't have to answer all the questions if I chose not to. Instead, I could simply reply 'No comment'.

After a couple of hours, I was taken into an interview room where two detectives sat behind a table with a tape recorder on it. I sat down next to the duty solicitor, feeling apprehensive.

The older detective flicked a button on the tape recorder, noted the date and time and then said, 'So, you know why you're here?'

I nodded. 'Yeah.'

'Okay, tell us what happened,' he said.

'The taxi driver stole my wallet.'

'The taxi driver said you called him an Asian bastard,' said the younger detective.

I was certain I hadn't used that phrase. However, I was painfully aware that I might have used another word, which I now know is a racial slur, but at the time I really didn't think of it like that. I'd grown up playing football, where throwing gratuitous abuse at your opponents was accepted as totally normal. It was always 'you fat bastard', 'you bald bastard', 'you old bastard'. In conflict or when drunk, you would select the first characteristic you observed and then use it as an insult. The same stuff had been thrown at me – especially 'fat bastard' in my younger days – and I didn't think anything of it. So I may well have referred to the driver as a 'Paki', but I genuinely didn't mean anything by it. To me, it was like calling someone from Scotland a Scot or someone from Wales a Taffy (even though I later discovered that the driver was from Bangladesh). And I hadn't called him an 'Asian bastard'.

'That's not true,' I told the detectives.

'Did you attack the driver because he was Asian?' said the older one.

'That had nothing to do with it.'

'Are you a racist?'

This was the point. I'd been drunk and angry, and I hadn't behaved well. But my anger was over the driver's actions, not his racial origins. 'Look, it wasn't racist… He took my wallet and he was trying to turn the car around.'

The driver had alleged I had attacked him for no reason, using racial abuse. So I gave my full account of the events. He had taken my wallet and refused to take me home. Why else was the taxi facing towards Leicester rather than Market Harborough?

The younger detective then read out a statement from a witness who said he'd seen me punching the driver.

'Is this true?' asked the older detective.

The solicitor leaned towards me and whispered that I should reply 'No comment'. I followed his advice.

At the end of the interview, I was charged with assault occasioning actual bodily harm and racially aggravated assault occasioning actual bodily harm. Hearing those words read out sent a shock through me. There was no way I was a racist. As far as I knew, I'd never behaved in a racist way against anyone in my life.

After a five-minute break, my interviewers moved onto the fake currency business. By now, those seventeen notes had been discovered in my car. I refused to tell the police where I'd obtained the notes, as I didn't want to drop the shopkeeper in it. Thinking creatively, I said I'd been given the money by someone for whom I did building work. He had threatened me if I disclosed his name.

Two days later, I appeared at Leicester Magistrates' Court and pleaded not guilty to the charges relating to the incident with the taxi driver. I elected to go to crown court because I was adamant that I wasn't guilty and I felt confident that a jury would realise this. I wanted to go in the witness box and tell my story. Of course, I shouldn't have punched him, but if he'd taken me to Harborough, it wouldn't have happened.

As for the other matter, I went to see a solicitor, and he told me that being in possession of counterfeit notes was regarded as a serious offence; spending them was even more serious. On that charge, I pleaded guilty at Leicester Magistrates' Court. The judge gave me one hundred and forty hours' community service.

When you get a community service order, you are often

sent to work in charity shops or old people's homes. At first I wasn't allowed to, because I had a pending charge for an alleged violent offence. I was told I had to work at a community centre in Leicester and be there at nine o'clock every Monday morning. (Community service tends to be one day a week, so you can carry on earning a living.) This meant leaving the house at 7.30am and taking two buses. If you were one minute late, they would close the door and refuse to let you in. I would finish at the community centre at 5pm. My duties included litter-picking and painting walls. Eventually they allowed me to work in a charity shop in Market Harborough, unpacking donations and ironing, which I found slightly easier, but community service certainly wasn't a soft option for me. I've heard people say, in all sincerity, that they would rather go to prison for a few weeks, and get it over and done with, than do two hundred hours of community service.

In one of the few good things to happen at this time, I started going out with Sally. I'd sometimes pick her up in the taxi from the Nags Head, where she worked behind the bar. I learned that she had grown up on a farm in the nearby village of Gumley and loved horse-riding, and she had taken part in lots of show-jumping events. Her father, who was a dairy farmer, had stables and lots of horses. She'd been in a long-term relationship and had two children, Bonnie and Robbie. I eventually invited her on a date. Even though we came from very different backgrounds, we hit it off and we started going out with each other.

Little did I know the important part Sally was to play in my life, and in helping me achieve the success that was to come.

6

ONLY 120 DAYS TO GO

AND SO IT WAS THAT, a year after the incident in the taxi, I found myself in the dock at Leicester Crown Court for my sentencing hearing, listening to the judge tell me I had to spend the next eight months in prison.

Still stunned by his words, I was taken back down to the cells to wait for the prison van, which would arrive at the end of the day. Because I wasn't expecting this sentence, I hadn't packed any clothes or toiletries when I left the house that morning.

My mum and dad were allowed to come and see me, but they had to talk to me through a glass screen.

'Oh, James, this is terrible,' murmured my mum, wiping tears from her eyes.

'Don't worry, only a hundred and twenty days to go,' said my dad, jokingly.

'Thanks for that, Dad.'

At around five o'clock, I was handcuffed and led outside

into the yard at the back of the court, then shoved into a prison van and taken the short distance to HMP Leicester, a Victorian building on Welford Road. I'd passed it many times and always thought that, with its turrets and formidable entrance, it looked like a castle. But castles are designed to keep people out; this building was fortified to keep us in.

After the van pulled into the courtyard at the prison, I was led through a door into an area where I had to take off all my clothes to be strip-searched. I was given prison clothes and then taken to see a doctor, who asked me what I was addicted to.

'Nothing,' I said, wondering how unusual this answer was.

I was then taken to the arrivals' suite, which had a pool table. I stood there with a small group of other prisoners, waiting to be taken to the wing and wondering what awaited me. By this time, I was scared stiff. To try to alleviate my anxiety, I got talking to two Asian lads in the queue. They both said they were fraudsters. One was called Beejay and the other, a stocky guy with a beard, Jazz.

You were only allowed one phone call, so I called Sally. She asked me if I was okay. I said I was, even though I was petrified about what life would be like inside the prison. Sally and her two girls started crying on the phone.

I was put into a cell with Jazz. He asked me why I'd been sent to prison, and I told him. It seemed odd that, having been convicted of a racist offence, I was put in a cell with an Asian guy. Thankfully, he was cool about it.

The next morning, the prison chaplain visited the cell to ask how I was and make sure I wasn't feeling suicidal. I told him I didn't have those kinds of thoughts.

Then a prison officer came to see me and explained that I was a Category D prisoner.

'What does that mean?' I asked.

'You're not seen as dangerous. A lot of the guys in here are. That's why we're a Cat B.'

'I understand.'

'You still might have to serve your sentence here, though.'

'Yeah?'

'But we'll try and get you moved to a Cat D prison as soon as possible.'

His words gave me a lift.

I was then taken to a wing, which looked just like those I'd seen on TV. Walking through it felt incredibly scary. Some of the prisoners were shouting, screaming or banging on their cell doors. I was put in a cell with Glyn, a tall guy in his early forties with lots of tattoos. No introductions, or anything; you're just pushed into the cell and left to get on with it. When I sat down on the edge of my bed, I noticed a cockroach scurrying across the floor. On the walls were lots of pictures Glyn had drawn; most were of the devil having sex with people.

'Do you like them?' he asked.

'Yeah, they're great,' I lied.

'Really?'

'I love them.'

Glyn, I learned, was a career criminal who had been involved in burglaries, robberies and drugs. He filled me in on what to do and not do in the prison. He told me there was an unwritten rule among prisoners that you didn't go for a shit in the toilet in the cell. You waited until you were let out in the morning when you could use the toilet block. He warned me to stay out of the showers, as they could be dangerous. But I also worried that Glyn might be dangerous. He'd be lying on his bed and then jump up and start screaming out of the window. When I did some exercises in the cell, which involved dropping onto my front and jumping back up again, he told me I was mental. I said I was just trying to keep fit. He couldn't understand it.

Breakfast was delivered to the cell. You went down to get your lunch and evening meal and then took a tray back to your cell and put it through the hatch afterwards. The cell would be locked at 8.30pm.

Apart from going out for the two meals and forty-five minutes' exercise in the yard, I wasn't allowed out of the cell for four days because there was a staff shortage. I was given some adventure paperbacks, which helped to take my mind off the situation I was in.

I spent much of the time lying on my bed thinking about what I was going to do with the rest of my life. The truth was I didn't know. I was still in shock at my incarceration. I realised I could quite easily have killed the taxi driver. If he'd had a weapon, I might have managed to take it from him and hit him with it. This thought chilled me.

The next day, I was given a job rolling posters in a workshop. While I was there, I heard lots of shouting and swearing from the windows. When I asked another prisoner what it was all about, he said it was because some 'nonces' were walking around the exercise yard; sex offenders were segregated from other prisoners.

I witnessed several fights and I heard about prisoners trying to commit suicide. It was a scary place and there was always tension in the air. You had to queue to use the phone, and some prisoners would push in and arguments would break out. I did my best to steer clear of any potential conflict and keep myself to myself.

There had been a riot at Lincoln prison and some of its inmates had been sent to Leicester. I got talking to one of them, who said he'd had something to do with the three drug dealers who were shot dead in a Range Rover in Essex in 1995. The story was told in the film *The Essex Boys*.

On the Thursday morning, a prison officer opened the door of my cell.

'You're leaving in the morning, mate,' he said.

'Where am I going?' I said.

'North Sea Camp.'

'Where's that?'

'Near Boston in Lincolnshire. It's a Cat D. It's much cushier than here.'

I sighed with relief. The prospect of serving all my sentence in a hellhole such as Leicester had terrified me.

Early on Friday morning, I was taken from my cell, handcuffed then escorted out of the prison and put into a van to take me to North Sea Camp. I peered through the small window at people shopping and chatting in the street, going about their daily business. They were doing such routine, ordinary things, with no idea that I was watching them enviously. And then we were heading through countryside. I saw a farm, a tractor ploughing a field, a church spire, an inviting old pub. All of this was part of normal life. A life I had taken for granted. Now, my freedom had been taken away. I no longer got to choose what I did. Others were deciding that for me.

I had no idea what to expect of North Sea Camp but, when I was led out of the van, I understood why it was called an open prison. It was nothing like HMP Leicester. At the entrance there was just a barrier, like in a car park, and there was no perimeter wall or razor wire. And instead of being a grim fortress, it was a collection of small buildings laid out between pathways and lawns, with fields beyond.

After being processed, I was given two pairs of jogging bottoms and some T-shirts and jumpers, along with underwear and socks. I was then taken to a single-storey building called South Unit 1. To my surprise, prisoners had rooms rather than cells: there were no bars on the windows, every prisoner had his own key, which meant you could come and go, and the room had its own TV and kettle. It wasn't unlike my RAF dormitory. Initially I shared the room with a quietly spoken guy, but he was moved to another room after a couple of days.

The canteen served three meals a day, and you had plenty of choice, such as minced beef and onion pie, chicken curry and rice, fish burgers and savoury pancakes. We had to fill in a pink sheet and hand it in the week before, to say what we wanted. I was training hard and I was trying to make good choices about the food I ate in order to keep fit, so I often ordered a salad.

Each morning at 7.30am, we all had to go to the guards' office for the first of several daily roll calls. After breakfast in the canteen, you went to do the job you had been allocated. Most prisoners either worked on the farm or as cleaners. Because I was doing a degree, I got a job in the education centre, helping other prisoners with basic maths and English.

I was curious about how the prison got its name. A prison officer told me it had opened in 1935 as a borstal, and the inmates initially lived on a campsite while permanent buildings were constructed. During this time, they helped to build a wall to protect the site from the North Sea.

The prison allowed me to continue with my studies at University College Northampton. When I was sentenced, I was a week or two away from my exams. The university got in touch with the prison authorities and all my books were sent to me. I was given time to revise for my exams, which were scheduled for September, and to do coursework.

I thought I'd be eligible for a tag and would only have to serve eight weeks at North Sea Camp. However, I discovered that the rules had changed just a few months earlier. Racist and sexual assaults, as well as some other crimes, no longer qualified for a tag. I was devastated when I heard this.

The atmosphere at North Sea Camp felt quite relaxed and laid back. People seemed to like it there because it was a lot easier than being in a prison such as Leicester. Nevertheless, several fights took place in the TV room. We had Sky Sports on the TV. I don't remember any Leicester games but I remember watching Manchester United vs Arsenal in the match that became known as the 'Battle of Old Trafford'. People would sometimes get dragged into the TV room and beaten up. From what I could make out, this was usually over drug debts. There was a lot of drug-taking in the prison. If you got up in the middle of the night to go to the toilet, you would sometimes see guys spaced out on drugs. I was never threatened during my time at North Sea Camp, although on one occasion the guy in the room next to mine complained that I was making noise at night. He got very angry with me. I apologised and said maybe I was accidentally hitting the wall when I rolled over. To avoid any further confrontations, I moved my bed away from the wall.

Sometimes prisoners would go out of the prison to collect packages of drugs that people had left for them, and you'd see prison officers chasing them. It was a game of cat and mouse until they got caught. Occasionally, the rooms would be ripped to pieces because prison officers were looking for drugs.

I spoke to several guys who told me they were in for burglary. To them, going to prison was just part of the job. Others had found their way there for much more unexpected reasons. For example, one of my neighbours was Gary Hart, who had fallen asleep at the wheel of his Land Rover near Selby in North Yorkshire in 2001 and, after drifting off the motorway, crashed down an embankment and ended up on the East Coast Main line. As he was phoning 999, his Land Rover was hit by the Newcastle to London train, which was then hit by a freight train. Eight people were killed and eighty injured. He was convicted of causing death by dangerous driving.

Then there were people who were in for drug dealing and VAT or tax fraud, and others coming to the end of their sentences, such as Phil, who had been sentenced to eighteen months for racially aggravated harassment after sending emails to a Jewish BBC radio presenter. And when the author and politician Jeffrey Archer was convicted of perjury and perverting the course of justice, he served part of his four-year sentence at North Sea Camp, where he worked in the medical centre. He was released not long before I arrived.

When someone told you why they were in prison, you could never be sure if they were telling the truth. If someone was in because of sexual abuse, for example, they wouldn't tell you; they'd make something else up instead.

Sally used to write to me every day. When I was sent down, she took it really hard and so did her daughters. It wasn't easy for her when I was in prison. She was holding down two jobs and I was asking her to send me money so that I could buy phone cards and go to the shop on a Saturday morning. I would buy a bottle of orange squash, which would last me a week. And I would buy seven tins of tuna, seven packets of noodles and packets of Nice biscuits.

Sally came to visit me twice a week, on Wednesdays and Sundays, which meant driving two hours there and two hours back. Sometimes she'd bring my mum or my dad. Some of my friends came a couple of times. I said I didn't want any visits on Saturdays because I played football.

We met in the visiting room. During Sally's first visit, I got up to go to the loo because I'd drunk four cans of Diet Coke in quick succession. As I approached the door, two prison officers grabbed hold of me.

'What the hell do you think you're doing?' said one of them.

'I'm just going to the toilet,' I replied.

'You're not allowed to do that.'

'Honestly, I didn't know. It's my first visit.'

'Sit back down.'

After the first couple of weeks, I became eligible for day release once a week, but I would have to be back by 7pm. On the first occasion, Sally picked me up and we drove to Skegness, where we booked a hotel room. But it all felt a bit weird. I didn't feel myself. We walked along the promenade, had something to eat in a café and I spoke about my plans after prison.

When Buzz had heard I'd been convicted, he wrote to me asking if I'd still be paying rent for the flat. I told him I couldn't afford it and said he could get someone else for my room. Stevie moved in.

Buzz wrote to me regularly, trying to cheer me up. He filled me in on stuff that had been happening since I was sent down. He said the Real Lions were missing me, as they were bottom of the league and needed a new striker. I smiled when I read this, as Jordie, our striker, was pretty rubbish. He told me he'd splashed out on a new Sony TV, DVD player, Sky box and a microwave. The *Harborough Mail* had run a story about me being sent to prison, but, thankfully, it hadn't made me out to be a racist. The last thing I wanted after prison was for everyone to label me as that. Buzz also told me that he, Stevie and Friz had applied for visiting orders to come and see me.

I gave up on trying to see Hannah. Charlotte and her mother could use my conviction to prove I wasn't a fit father. I thought about Hannah a lot, though, and hoped that when she was older, I would be able to see her again.

Beejay and Jazz, whom I'd met in Leicester prison, also got sent to North Sea Camp, and I ended up sharing a room with Beejay. I learned that he had grown up in Leicester and that he came from a well-to-do family; he had a posh accent and the gift of the gab. He told me he had been involved in tax and credit-card fraud. He used to go to the gym at 3.30pm every day to play badminton. He told me to say that I had a bad back, because then I would be allowed to go to the gym at 3.30pm instead of working until 5pm. This proved to be good advice. I did weights between 3.30pm and 5pm and then went to get changed and have dinner. Because I sweated in the gym, I found it difficult not being able to change my clothes that often.

Beejay and I would walk around the fields each day, talking about business ideas and what I was going to do when I got out of prison. My plan was to get a job in IT or business, but I wondered how likely this would be, given that I had a criminal record.

'James, you know what you should do when you get out?' said Beejay.

'What?' I said.

'Start your own business.'

'But I've been convicted of a racist attack.'

'It doesn't matter. You can still start a business.'

'In what?'

'What were you doing before you got sent down?'

'Just driving taxis.'

'There you are, then.'

'What do you mean?'

'Start a taxi business.'

'Taxis?'

'Yeah. There's money in it.'

'How? I'm skint.'

Beejay laughed. 'Listen, mate, it's easy to raise money.'

'But how?'

'Simple.'

'Go on.'

'Use credit cards.'

'You reckon?'

'Of course. See the money as a business loan.'

Beejay was one of those people who seem permanently full of optimism, and are always coming up with ideas. When you talked to him, he made you feel you could do anything.

In the evenings, I sometimes played pool or watched TV. I'd never watched TV soaps before, but I found myself becoming addicted to *EastEnders* and *Coronation Street*. Perhaps this was because they were about real life. I'd also go with Beejay to Jazz's room and we'd drink tea and play cards. Sundays were quiet. I played football in the morning and would then watch a Premier League match on TV in the afternoon.

I went out for a run one day around the football pitches and there was another guy running. We started to try to beat each other, even though neither of us said anything. His name was Pav. I got chatting to him and after that I ended up training with him most days. I discovered that he had been given an eight-year sentence for importing drugs and was due to be released soon. He had lots of law books and was studying to be a solicitor. He used to go out to work and sometimes he'd bring me back a pot of protein from Holland & Barrett. I would get Sally to send him twenty quid.

I started playing for the prison football team. We would train every weekday evening and have a game among ourselves at 6.30pm. We'd play football until about eight and then come in and sign in at the office. The team played in the Lincolnshire league. For obvious reasons, we didn't play away; all our games were played at the prison on Saturdays. Usually, about two hundred prisoners would come to watch the games. I think the other teams enjoyed coming to the prison to play.

The manager of the football team was a prison officer who happened to be a really good coach. He drummed into us that we had to be disciplined and that if anyone stepped out of line they wouldn't play any more. So we never gave any backchat to the referees. I've played for a few football managers, but none of them were able to give a team confidence in the way he could. He never told you off if you made a mistake on the pitch; he was more about encouragement. The right-back was serving seventeen years for murder. One of the defenders had killed someone when drink-driving. The centre-forward, who had gold teeth, had picked up cocaine for someone and been ambushed by the police. Despite the chequered background of the players, it was the best football team I've ever played in. We won every game during my time in the team.

Being a member of the football team at the prison was held in high regard. You would often be treated better; for example, you might get an extra sausage in the canteen. In prison, small things like this matter a lot.

My sentence came to an end in September 2003. I promised to meet up with Beejay when he got out. I had to wait in a queue to be processed. I was asked about my state of mind and whether I felt ready for release. The truth was, I'd never felt so excited. All night I'd been looking forward to being reunited with friends and family, to being able to do what I wanted, without ever again taking my freedom for granted, and to start making something of my life. That's not why they were asking, of course. For plenty of prisoners, especially those who have spent much longer in the system than I had, returning to the outside world can be a terrifying business, particularly if they don't have family support and have nowhere to live. Fortunately, that wasn't the case for me. After filling out a lot of forms, I was handed a plastic bag containing my own clothes. Outside, Sally was waiting for me. On the drive back to Market Harborough we stopped at McDonald's. A Big Mac had never tasted so good.

That was on the Wednesday. Three days later, I was back. Not because I'd messed up – but to play for the football team in a big game. Once more, we won. Afterwards, I went to a local pub for a few drinks with the coach, his son, who was also a prison officer and played in the team, and a couple of other prison officers. We talked mainly about football. At the end of the evening, the coach wished me well for the future, and I thanked him for being such a good football coach.

I was at North Sea Camp during a warm summer. The fifteen weeks I spent there might have been very different if it had been a dark winter, because I wouldn't have been able to play football as much as I did. Being a member of that team helped me to survive prison. When I got out, I even considered going back to North Sea Camp every week so I could carry on playing, but I eventually decided that driving there and back would be too much hassle. I felt lucky to have served most of my time in that prison. Had I remained at Leicester, who knows what might have happened to me.

My time in prison led me to think about whether the justice system works. As far as I could see, some people – the burglars, for example – weren't interested in being rehabilitated: after their release, they would continue to commit crime, seeing imprisonment as an occupational hazard. Men like that had chosen house-breaking as a career path because they thought there were no better options for them. On the other hand, there are those who use prison as an opportunity to change their lives, like Pav.

In my case, prison was also about to bring about a huge change. But I could never have guessed in those early days after my release just how big or how positive this would turn out to be.

7

TAXI WARS

BEING FREE AGAIN FELT AMAZING. I soon settled back into life in Market Harborough, spending lots of time with my parents, Tom and my friends. I moved in with Sally at her house in Fairfax Road.

I can't say if some people in the town viewed me as a violent person or as a racist. All I know is that the incident with the taxi driver was out of character for me. People close to me knew that. I was determined to put it behind me and get on with my life.

I wasn't sure what I should do. I needed to earn some money, as I was totally skint. The chats with Beejay about running my own business had inspired me, and I felt confident that I could do it. My dad had always told me that achieving anything in life was all about hard work, and I definitely had the motivation to do something. I just didn't know what.

As I still had my taxi licence, I decided to follow Beejay's advice to the letter and start a taxi company. I understood how that business worked and I felt I could make a success of it. Using my credit cards and a bank loan I took out with the Alliance & Leicester, I was able to buy a Ford Mondeo and a Ford Focus for £2,000 each, and I got them licensed with Harborough District Council.

One of Beejay's many useful instructions was to come up with a catchy name for the company that people would remember. There was a cab firm in Corby called Busy Bees, so I decided to call my own company Spotty Dog. It was memorable, and my mum had told me that when I was three, I was frightened to go to sleep because I thought there was a spotty dog under the bed, so it had personal significance for me. I would have spots sprayed on the cars to make them distinctive.

Sally and Tom both agreed to become taxi drivers and applied to the council for licences. My dad had been driving taxis ever since losing his screen-printing business in the mid-1990s. He had worked for both of Market Harborough's taxi companies, Murphy's and Kwik Cabs. I guaranteed him a certain amount of money each week if he'd drive for Spotty Dog.

The company launched in November 2003, less than two months after I left prison. I had worked my socks off to get it up and running. I couldn't afford to rent an office, so I ran the firm from a mobile phone.

There were two types of taxi licences: hackney carriage and private hire. Hackney carriage taxis could sit on the rank, but private hire had to be booked. The taxi I drove had a hackney carriage licence. A plate displayed next to the number plate gave the licence number, which meant that if anyone had a complaint, they could take the number of the taxi.

We were only licensed to pick people up within the boundaries of Harborough District Council. If you took a customer to Leicester, for example, you weren't allowed to pick up any customers there. Despite this, I would hang around, waiting for a fare. If the licensing team at Harborough District Council were to catch me, I'd be in trouble, but I was prepared to take the risk to try to maximise revenue.

We did lots of airport jobs; we charged £35 for East Midlands, £40 for Birmingham, £55 for Luton, £75 for Heathrow and £95 for Gatwick. We also won several council contracts to do school runs in the mornings and afternoons. These are good business for taxi firms because they provide guaranteed income. I also did regular jobs for Gartree prison. Usually, this would involve taking prisoners under guard to family funerals, or prison officers to Leicester Royal Infirmary to take over from another officer who was on suicide watch with a prisoner. Another nice job was picking up staff from KFC in Market Harborough. They paid the same fare as everyone else but they'd always give us some chicken and fries.

We soon became really busy, running cars twenty hours a day. That meant we were constantly exhausted. On one occasion, I fell asleep at a junction. At other times, I had to slap myself around the face to stay awake. To stop myself falling asleep, I'd drive with the windows down in all weathers, and the radio on, necking cans of Red Bull.

I tried to never let a customer down. If someone phoned me at 11pm asking me to take them to the railway station at 5.30 the next morning, when I'd been hoping for a lie-in, I'd agree to do it, even if the fare was only three quid. It meant the company built up a reputation for being always available. This reliability obviously translated into more business, because we were the first company many people phoned.

Eventually, I rented a small office next to the Broadway nightclub and we'd park the cars outside it. We recruited drivers from Kwik Cabs and Murphy's who preferred to work for us as our phones were always ringing. I also hired a bookkeeper, whom I met when I picked him up one day to take him to the station.

The average taxi driver was an overweight guy in his forties. Some of them wanted it nice and easy and just worked Monday to Friday, while others worked at weekends only or all the hours they could get. If a driver was in one of our cars, the fare would be split sixty-forty in our favour. If it was their own car, it would be an eighty-twenty split in their favour. Back then, it was all cash fares, which made it easy for anyone who decided to fiddle. Some fares weren't recorded by drivers, so they could make more money. And some didn't declare all of their income to HMRC. A few of the drivers were hard work: they were either not quite all there or they were always phoning in sick.

While Micky Adams was manager of Leicester City, he started using our taxis. Any time he phoned me, I'd always fit him in. After he left Leicester and joined Coventry City in January 2005, he booked me to take him and a small group of friends to Brighton, where he was having his stag party. I hired an eight-seater. One of Micky's friends was Alan Cork, who had played over four hundred games for Wimbledon and scored nearly two hundred goals; he was Micky's number two at Leicester.

When we arrived in Brighton, we booked into the Grand Hotel on the seafront. Several ex-Brighton players met up with us and we went to a few pubs in the centre of the city. Micky had been manager of Brighton & Hove Albion before joining Leicester. Under his leadership, Brighton had won the third-division title and been promoted to the second division. Everywhere we went, people made a huge fuss of Micky and we were all given VIP treatment. At the end of the night, we all staggered back to the Grand, by which time I was really drunk. For some reason, I started trying to play the piano. I'd never played a piano in my life. Micky and everyone else thought it was hilarious.

The following morning, I met Micky and his friends on the beach. They were already drinking. I thought I'd have a couple of Budweisers, but I drank more than a couple, somehow managing to completely forget that I had to drive back to Leicester. Fortunately, Alan Cork proved to be a legend in private as well as on the pitch. Realising that I was too drunk to drive, he said he'd get behind the wheel. I slept in the back all the way home.

I was now turning out regularly for Harborough Town, whose ground was on Northampton Road, behind the leisure centre, and who played in the Northants Combination Premier Division. Sometimes I'd play for the first team and sometimes for the reserves. I usually played in defence, but occasionally I'd be told by the manager to go up front, and when I did, I often scored a goal or created one. In the end, though, I was on the bench a lot, and the manager got rid of me. I then played for Borough Alliance as a centre-forward. During my time, we won the league and one of the cups.

Back at work, Spotty Dog was the new boy in town and we were taking lots of work from the other taxi companies. The local newspaper ran a headline about 'taxi wars' in Harborough. After coming out of prison, I'd driven for both Kwik Cabs and Murphy's, who both knew about my criminal record. Now one or more of their drivers wrote to the council to tell them about that record. In March 2004, I was called to a meeting with several councillors at Harborough District Council offices. They told me that because I hadn't informed them about my conviction, they were suspending my licence. It made no difference that I'd obtained the licence before I went to prison; they said I should have updated them when my circumstances changed. The company could still operate, but I could no longer be a driver.

By now, we had seven or eight cars. As a result of the council's decision, we lost all our contracts for school runs, as well as a few drivers. Unable to work, I spent a lot of my time training and playing football. I played for Desborough in the UCL, then Harborough in the Northants Combination League. As I had so much time on my hands, I sometimes played football six days a week. But I also appealed against the council's decision, which I didn't think was fair. My appeal was successful and the council gave me back my licence. However, we never got the school runs back, or the drivers who had left, so the business was never the same again.

I was restless to do something else. But what?

Having achieved a 2:1 in my degree, I returned to University College Northampton for my graduation ceremony. I sat in the crowded hall, wearing the traditional cap and gown, with Sally and my dad, waiting for my name to be called out. When I heard it, I walked purposefully to the front to shake hands with the chancellor, feeling a huge sense of achievement. I'd been in the RAF in the first year, in prison during the second and building the taxi business in the final year. But I had still managed to get a good degree.

By way of celebration, I decided to go to the 2004 Euro Championships with Buzz and Tom. Sally agreed to run Spotty Dog while I was away. I'd heard on the news that known troublemakers were going to be prevented from travelling, but it never occurred to me that this might be an issue for me. While checking in at Birmingham airport for the flight to Faro, I felt a tap on my shoulder. I looked around to see a man in plain clothes who introduced himself as a detective.

'You need to come with me,' he said.

'Why?' I said.

'You've been identified as a potential football hooligan.'

He led me through the crowded terminal to an office and told me to sit down.

'It's very unlikely you're going to be allowed to travel,' he said.

'Why not?'

'Because of your conviction for violence.'

'But that was ages ago, and it was nothing to do with football. I'm not going to Portugal to cause trouble. I'm just going to watch England.'

'I'll have to speak to my superintendent, and he'll make the decision. You'll need to wait here.'

He left the office and I sat there thinking that was it. Buzz and Tom would have to go on their own and I'd have to go back to Market Harborough. I couldn't believe this was happening. But when the detective returned, he said, to my surprise, that I was free to travel. My trip was back on.

After arriving at Faro, we hired an eight-seater minibus. We spent a couple of nights in an apartment in the middle of Albufeira, the resort town on the Algarve coast. The apartment was on the main strip, which was lined with bars and clubs.

England's first group game was against France in Lisbon. Frank Lampard put England one nil up and then Beckham missed a penalty. France won 2–1 when Zidane scored a penalty in the last minute.

We returned to Albufeira and went to La Bamba bar, just below our apartment, to have a drink. We sat outside on the edge of the street. There were lots of other England fans around, but, despite the fact that we had lost, the atmosphere seemed happy. Across the street a number of police with riot shields stood watching. Then I heard glass smash and bottles came flying over my head towards the police. The next minute, they drew their batons and charged across the road towards us, hitting out at everyone, whether we were involved in the trouble or not. People began to scatter. Tables were turned upside down and glasses were smashed. It was total carnage. One of the officers whacked Tom across the leg. We fled down the street with the police chasing us. I jumped over a fence.

The police cordoned off the strip, closed all the bars and we weren't allowed to go back to our apartment for a couple of hours. We'd just wanted a good night out, but some idiots had put an end to that by throwing bottles at the police.

We'd planned to go to a water park the following morning. When we got downstairs, the reception area looked like a war zone. Outside, there were TV crews in the street. I did an interview for Sky News, and Tom showed his bruises to the camera.

The following evening, we went to La Bamba bar again, but this time we sat a table at the back rather than by the edge of the street, in case trouble kicked off again. Sure enough, it did. A group of England fans began hurling bottles at the police. The police charged, just like the night before. England fans, wearing shorts and flip-flops, fought back. The police promptly shut down all the bars again, so another night was ruined.

The next day, we drove north to Coimbra, in the centre of the country, for the game against Switzerland. We arrived at around 7pm and went to find a hotel, but each one we tried was fully booked. We'd have to spend the night in the minibus – a prospect that that none of us was keen on. Climbing back in, we drove around looking for a place to park up for the night. We found a busy street with lots of cars already parked, but enough space for the minibus, so we left it there and went to a bar, which was showing the Portugal vs Russia game on TV. We got some drinks and sat down to watch. During the evening, we got chatting to another group of England fans. When we told them we weren't able to find a hotel, they said we could have a shower in the morning at their rented apartment. It turned out these guys were a Housemartins tribute band. After the game, they invited us to a club, where Norman Cook, better known as Fatboy Slim, was deejaying. We had a fantastic night and didn't get back to the minibus until about 3am.

Just after seven, I was woken up by knocking on the window. I looked up to see the face of a policeman. I opened the door and asked what the problem was. He said we had parked on a roundabout. All the other vehicles had gone and we were the only ones there. The policeman told us we needed to park in a side street. Afterwards, we went to the tribute band's apartment, showered and then went to the match, which England won 3–0, with two goals scored by Wayne Rooney, who was only eighteen, and one by Steven Gerrard. Things were looking up.

We drove back to Albufeira and booked into a hotel. This time, we didn't see any trouble. We spent three days in the resort, going to the beach each morning and the bars in the evening. We then headed to Lisbon for the final group game, against Croatia. Thousands of England fans were milling around in the centre of the city. England went behind in the fifth minute but ended up winning 4–2, with Rooney scoring twice again and Scholes and Lampard also getting on the score sheet. After the game, we made our way to the docks and went to a bar which played English songs all evening. A Portuguese

TV crew turned up and started buying people pints of lager, which they then wanted them to down in one, so they could film them doing it; obviously their aim was to show how crazy the England fans were.

England were due to play Portugal in the quarter-final, and I didn't want to go home. The flight I'd booked back to Birmingham was due to leave during the match. But we'd come all this way to see England; we couldn't possibly leave now and not see them in the quarter-final.

I phoned Sally to tell her I was thinking of staying for the Portugal game. She was stressed out. One of the drivers had left and another had had an accident, so she was having to drive as well as run the office. She said if I didn't come back, she'd leave me. I had no option but to return. I could see it wasn't fair to leave her on her own. I managed to get an earlier flight that day and got back to Market Harborough in time to watch the match at the Talbot. England lost on penalties. Had Rooney not broken his foot and had to go off, we might have won.

Going to the Euros had provided a much-needed break from running Spotty Dog. The company was doing okay, but there were constant problems. Taxis were always breaking down and some of the drivers were not the brightest sparks and were hard work. Sometimes you'd think you had a night off and then one of them would ring in saying he was sick; maybe he was, maybe he wasn't, but there wasn't anything you could do about it. On Saturday nights there would be taxi inspections, and you might be told that one of your tyres was defective or there was a problem with one of your lights, so you'd be ordered to take your car off the road. We'd also bought a minibus and a new six-seater Ford Galaxy, a lovely car, but one of the drivers crashed the Galaxy. Although we had it repaired, it was never really right again, losing us about twenty grand.

By this time my friend Friz had left the Royal Navy and gone backpacking around Australia with Buzz, taking casual jobs in mobile phone sales. After he returned to Market Harborough, he had set up a telesales company selling corporate hospitality, and by all accounts he was doing really well. He had a call centre and was making a lot of money, buying tickets for events such as Royal Ascot and Wimbledon and selling them at a higher price.

For me, working seven days a week and putting in about eighty hours, selling corporate hospitality tickets sounded like an easier way of making money than driving taxis. I had installed a BT feature line in the office, even though I didn't know what I would do with it: it had four telephone lines on the same number. I needed to do something else with my life, and maybe this was the key to it.

8

MAKING THE SWITCH

ONE COLD SATURDAY NIGHT in October, I picked up a guy called Gavin Williams in the square in Market Harborough to take him to the top of the town. He was probably twenty-two, so six years younger than me. When you're a taxi driver, you always get customers who want to talk. Gavin was one of them. I can't remember how it came about, but he started telling me about the energy market. He explained that after leaving school he'd gone to catering college and worked as a cook for a while, but, because he didn't like it, he now had a job in sales in Leicester.

'I've just started working with a company called Economy Power,' he said.

'I can't say I've heard of them.'

'It's an energy supplier.'

'Like British Gas?'

'Yeah, but they deal with electricity.'

'What's your job?'

'I'm what you call an energy broker.'

'A kind of middleman, then?'

'You got it.'

'So how do you make your money?'

'Economy Power will pay either five hundred quid or three hundred and fifty quid for every new business I sign up.'

'Yeah?'

'I'm serious. You can make proper money in energy switching.'

'Switching? How do you mean?'

'You know, getting a business to move from one supplier to another.'

'I never knew you could do that.'

'A lot of people don't. Do you fancy getting involved?'

'I dunno. I mean, it sounds like good money.'

'Why don't you give it a go?'

'Okay, mate, I might do. Nothing to lose.'

If what Gavin said was true, this was an easier way to make decent money than driving a taxi all week, so I asked him to pop into the cab office at some point for a proper chat.

I didn't know anything about energy suppliers. It was a business that had never crossed my mind. But I reckoned it couldn't be too difficult to learn about it. From what Gavin had said, I could do just a few hours a week to begin with. If it really took off, then I could consider selling the taxi business.

The next day, Gavin turned up as promised at the cab office. He sat down next to me and produced contract packs, an impressively bound price book and various sheets of paper.

'What most people don't realise is that the cost of energy goes up and down,' he said, showing me a chart with lots of rows of numbers on it.

'You mean like mortgage rates?'

'Exactly.'

'Why does that happen?'

'Because suppliers like Economy Power buy it from whole-salers. It's all about the energy market.'

'I didn't know about that. I just thought energy came from East Midlands Electricity or whoever.'

'You see, energy suppliers charge consumers for each unit of gas or electricity they use, calculated as pence per kilowatt hour.'

'Kilowatt?' I recognised the term, but I'd never fully understood what it meant.

'Yeah, a kilowatt hour is a measure of how much energy you use per hour, whether it's boiling a kettle, lights, heating or whatever.'

'Okay, got you.'

'One kilowatt equals 1,000 watts. Depending on the tariff customers agree with their supplier, they might have more than one unit rate, for example day, night and weekend rates, which are shown separately on your bill.'

'How does the commission work?'

'It's simple. Energy suppliers include a commission in their unit rate.'

'What's the standing charge for, then?'

'That covers the cost of the pipes and power lines that supply the energy, and maintenance of meters and all that.'

'You mean like a line rental for a phone?'

'Exactly.'

He took out an Economy Power bill and, running his finger over it, explained all the information on it. 'You've got the customer account number, all the stuff about what you've paid previously and what you owe, the period of time the bill covers, what tariff you're on and, sometimes, when it ends. And here are the meter readings, the unit rate and the standing charge. Every electricity meter has a unique number. It's known as the electricity supply number or Meter Point Administration Number, MPAN for short. When you want to switch a customer, you have to have the MPAN and the information about what tariff they're on.'

He told me that he worked with an Economy Power accounts manager, Paul Johnson, who would authorise the commission. The only condition for customers was that they must spend at least £100 a month on energy. (If that doesn't sound much nowadays to the average domestic consumer, bear in mind that energy prices have since quadrupled.)

'Most people in business don't have a clue how their energy bills are worked out or know anything about kilowatts,' he said.

'Neither do I,' I said.

'This is where you can make good money, if you can get people to sign five-year contracts.'

'How do you do that?'

'You tell them you're saving them money.'

'And are you?'

'Definitely.'

'So how many contracts have you got, so far?'

Gavin explained that he'd previously worked for another energy broker, which was how he knew the business so well, but now he was setting up on his own. So far, he hadn't signed anyone up, but he was hoping he would have more success if I joined him in the venture.

'Okay, I'll give it a go,' I said. 'I've nothing to lose, have I?'

He smiled. 'No. And you might make some decent dosh.'

Gavin didn't have a car, so I picked him up at his house late one afternoon and we drove to Leicester. During the journey, he ran through what I had to do. He said we'd be targeting businesses such as restaurants, cafés, kebab shops and newsagents. He re-emphasised that we were only interested in signing businesses that spent at least a hundred quid a month on electricity. That was the Economy Power rule. While most business owners wouldn't have a clue how many kilowatts they used a month, they would know, roughly, how much money they paid.

'Why are we targeting these particular businesses?' I asked.

'Because they use a lot of energy; you know, they have cookers, fridges and all that.'

My job was to go in and ask to speak to the owner. If they were there, I'd then ask if they were interested in saving money on electricity bills. If they said yes, I'd ask to see their electricity bill and then say I was going to get a tariff check. I'd phone Gavin, who would be sitting in the car around the corner, telling the owner I was phoning head office. I'd give Gavin all the relevant information from the bill: the metre point reference number for gas or the MPAN for electricity, along with the tariff the customer was on. It might be a single rate, a day or night or a weekend rate. Gavin would give me a price, and I'd take out my calculator and work out how much the customer would save. If the customer was happy with it, I'd produce an Economy Power contract and direct debit mandate and ask him to sign them. Once he'd done that, I'd leave him copies along with my business card.

It felt odd when I spoke to the first business owners. Firstly, I'd never seen myself as a salesman, and, secondly, I knew nothing about energy switching, other than what Gavin had told me. I was a taxi driver, not an energy expert. Gavin had urged me to avoid answering too many questions. This was because Economy Power was a little bit sneaky. It said it was offering a fixed-term contract but after a few months the price would go up and there was nothing the customer could do about it because this information was hidden away in the terms and conditions.

After going out with Gavin for three evenings, we got our first deal at a bar on Churchgate, where the guy who had just bought it was doing a refurbishment. Gavin said new owners were likely to be open to switching suppliers.

'Yeah, I'm interested,' he said. 'We all want to save money.'

After I'd phoned Gavin, I said something like, 'The standing charge is forty-five pence a day and the unit rate is ten pence.'

'How cheap is that compared to what I'm on?' asked the owner.

'You'd save about three grand a year.'

'Which company is it?'

'Economy Power.'

'And I'd save that much money?'

'Yeah, more or less.'

'Okay then, I'll change to it.'

The following day, I popped into a newsagent to buy a can of Diet Coke. Opening the door, I heard the owner complaining to someone on the phone about his electricity bill. I thought, *I might get a sale here.* When he came off the phone, I introduced myself and explained how I could save him money on his electricity bill. I left the shop with another contract.

I learned about the energy business on the job, which is often the best way. I was only one page ahead of the customers most of the time. I quickly discovered that getting a customer to switch wasn't all plain sailing. Once a customer had signed a contract, I'd send it by recorded delivery to Economy Power's office in Manchester. Economy Power would then apply to take over from the existing supplier. However, if a customer was already in contract, a supplier could object. Most customers didn't know if they were in contract or not. If they were, we wouldn't receive a commission. Some customers might be in debt, which meant they couldn't switch until they'd paid it off. Also, a customer might phone their existing supplier and say they'd signed a contract with Economy Power but had changed their mind and ask for a better rate. So we might get ten contracts in a week, but three or four of them might not go through.

Going door to door to try to find customers was time-consuming, so I gave two of the girls who worked in the Spotty Dog office copies of the Leicester edition of the *Yellow Pages* and asked them to start phoning businesses to try to book appointments for me and Gavin. We had five phone lines in the office. My brother Tom and two mates, Johnny and Matt, also came on board. Gavin provided basic training in what to say to customers.

We formed a company called Business Energy Consultants Ltd, the name Gavin had been using when he introduced himself to customers, and registered it at Companies House. However, Tom, Johnny and Matt all decided that this kind of business wasn't for them and they quit.

Even though Gavin and I didn't really know what we were doing, and were making mistakes all the time, the business began to grow. Most weeks, we were getting five contracts.

It soon reached the point where it was no longer feasible to operate from the cab office, so we rented a small serviced office on Coventry Road. The good thing about it was that the walls could be moved to create extra space. Because we didn't have much money, we kitted it out with second-hand furniture, some of it from the local council tip. If you saw something you wanted, you just gave one of the guys a few quid for it. It meant the office was like those trendy cafés you see everywhere nowadays: nothing matched. We were ahead of that curve, design-wise. We also bought a couple of computers.

I recruited Paul, my mum's partner, several other people I knew and a couple of students. Four of the team would be on the phones in the office trying to book seven appointments a day for the four of us who spent most of the time on the road. Gavin managed the team in the office and I managed those who were doing the appointments. The aim was to keep those appointments in one area of Leicester, so we weren't going from one side of the city to the other. Despite that attempt at efficiency, it was tough going and we had a lot of wasted journeys. You'd turn up at a restaurant or takeaway and the person you were due to meet wouldn't be there, or you were told they weren't available. All this wasted time came at a cost, not just in terms of what we were paying staff each week but also in petrol money. Everyone needed to be doing four or five deals a week for us to break even.

Gavin and I met regularly with Paul Johnson, the accounts manager at Economy Power, to discuss how things were going. A quietly spoken guy in his mid-forties, Paul epitomised the successful businessman: he drove a BMW, wore a smart suit with cufflinks and carried a gold pen. We'd usually meet him at the Enigma bar, opposite the office, at the Angel, or sometimes at a motorway service station. He always encouraged us to go for more sales and would offer tips on how to get them. Of course, the more sales we did, the more commission he earned.

One day, during a meeting with Paul at the Angel, he opened his leather briefcase and took out a small black box and placed it on the table.

'You don't need to be going out and seeing all these people,' he announced with a flourish.

'You've lost me,' I said.

'With this, people are doing hundreds of deals a week on the phone.'

'Yeah?'

Grinning, he picked up the black box. 'You see, all you have to do is plug this into the phone and your PC and then read a script out and record the call with the customer.'

'That's clever,' I said.

'It is, isn't it? You don't have to go door-knocking any more.'

'This is fantastic!' said Gavin. 'This means we can speak to fifty people a day instead of two.'

'That's the idea,' said Paul. 'Forget Leicester. You can go national now.'

My immediate reaction was to wonder how we would sell on the phone. But, I told myself, Paul seemed to know what he was talking about.

I told the staff that we were moving to telesales. Some of them said they didn't want to do this and handed in their notice.

Telesales isn't easy. You have to try to get the interest of a person straight away and also win their trust. Our opening line was, 'I'm calling from Business Energy Consultants. Would you like to save money on your electricity?' It was pretty basic. Gradually, we started building in FAQs.

We recorded the calls in case of any future disagreement about what the customer had or had not agreed to. We saved the phone recordings as WAV files and then sent them on a CD to Economy Power, along with the contracts. Some customers might be on a one-year contract, some on a five-year contract. We'd get five times the commission on a five-year deal, so we always tried to sell those instead of the one-year deals.

Our new system meant that we could now try to get business all over the country. In other words, we were evolving from a local company into a national one. Gavin's dad worked for the *Yellow Pages* and he got us discounted copies of directories for most towns and cities in the country. We'd phone cafés in the day and restaurants from 5pm onwards. We worked until seven or eight o'clock in the evening each day. It was relentless, but I knew that hard work usually pays off.

We began working with BizzEnergy and Total Gas and Power, who supplied both electricity and gas. It was easier to sell gas than electricity because we could access a UK database operated by Transco, now known as the National Grid, so that customers didn't need to pull out a bill. All we needed was the name of the business and the position in the company of the person we were speaking to.

With Economy Power, we had made between £350 and £500 per deal. When Total came on the scene, we made another £500–£1,500 commission, depending on how much energy the customer used. Now we were making £500 to £1,500 per customer if we sold them both gas and electricity. Soon we were doing fifteen or twenty deals a day and making decent money. I could see that we were on to something with a switching business. I knew I couldn't continue doing this and my taxi job for much longer, and I started to think about selling Spotty Dog.

Everything was running relatively smoothly until customers started to complain to Total Gas and Power, saying that they thought we were British Gas. Because our agents said they were calling about a customer's account with British Gas, customers often assumed that was the company they were from. It didn't help that we were calling people whose first language wasn't English. With Chinese restaurants, for example, the owners didn't always understand what they were agreeing to. Gavin and I now had to attend a meeting at Total's offices in

Redhill in Surrey. We explained that we hadn't tried to mislead people, but we admitted that maybe a few customers didn't really understand who we were. We were told to be clear about this with the customers. We realised with hindsight that we were sometimes mis-selling, although we didn't realise it. So we changed our practices.

In those days, the energy-switching business was like the Wild West. It was common for energy brokers to try to steal each other's customers. This was a relatively new sector and anything went. Although Ofgem existed, I don't think it fully understood what was going on in the energy brokering world.

In 2005, Business Energy Consultants moved to Fernie House, a converted warehouse on Fernie Road. We rented the top floor, which was big enough to accommodate up to sixty staff. Unlike the office on Coventry Road, this one had meeting rooms and a boardroom.

Because we were inexperienced, we didn't realise the implications of having our own office. We had to spend thousands on installing phone lines and carrying out other internal changes. Something else we hadn't considered was the poor state of the building. On hot days, Fernie House was unbearable. We'd sometimes let people go home because it was impossible to work in such heat, and have them come back in the evening. There was a time when we almost had siestas. If it rained, the roof leaked and we had to place rubbish bins around the office to catch the water. When you have lots of computers, this kind of situation isn't good.

Sally joined the company and started to organise all the admin. Neither Gavin nor I had paid sufficient attention to this side of the business, because we had been more focused on finding new customers, so it was all a bit chaotic. Sally began transferring all the customer details to Excel spread sheets and generally developing systems to make the company run more smoothly.

I wondered about branching out into telecommunications, as this was a growing market, so Gavin and I went to see a guy in Sheffield who ran a business selling phone contracts. Sid worked out of a shabby office in a run-down part of the city, but his sales guys were amazing. They stood at their desks all day long, banging the phones and smoking.

Sid and I discussed the possibility of a partnership where we would pass on details of our energy customers to him and he would pass on details of his phone customers to us. He said he'd send a guy called Doug Teskey to Market Harborough to provide our sales team with training in how to sell phone contracts.

The following week, Doug turned up at the Angel Hotel, where I'd hired a room for a day. He was a Canadian, who I discovered had been a professional ice hockey player for Toledo Storm in Ohio. He had come to the UK in 2004 to play, initially for Sheffield, but joined Newcastle Vipers. He'd quit hockey and gone to work in sales and marketing. I liked him immediately. He was charismatic and a fantastic communicator. His training session was brilliant. With his engaging smile, handsome looks and Canadian accent, he had the sales team hanging on his every word.

I'd booked Doug a room for the night at the hotel. We had a few drinks in the bar and chatted about business and our respective careers. Doug told me he was also making money from helping council tenants buy their properties under the right-to-buy scheme. Originally introduced by Margaret Thatcher, the scheme enabled tenants to purchase their home at a large discount. While Tony Blair's government had reduced the discounts, it was still an attractive deal. Doug was offering a service that took care of all the paperwork with the local council, mortgage company and solicitors, for which he received a commission.

He invited me to go out door-knocking with him to try to get some contracts. I said yes, as I thought this might be a lucrative business to move into. I took him to an area of the town with several streets of council houses, and we spent several hours knocking on doors. I'd been door-knocking at commercial premises, but this was my first experience of doing it in a residential area. I let Doug do all the talking. He knew how to connect with people. If a door was slammed in our faces, Doug just smiled and moved on. He was a natural when it came to sales.

I suggested to Gavin that we should offer Doug a job with the company. I felt his sales skills could really help us grow. Gavin agreed, so Doug joined the company and moved in with me and Sally.

I began thinking about investing in property and I talked to Doug about it. He said he was keen to do the same thing. We went to see some houses being built on a former mushroom farm at Middlebrook Green. We negotiated a price for two townhouses from £235,000 each to £208,000. The idea was for Doug to buy one of them and Sally and me to buy the other. I persuaded Sally to remortgage her house on Fairfax Road to raise the deposit. She and I then got a mortgage, but Doug was turned down. Not wanting to let the deal go, I bought the second property with a friend who worked in a bank, then I rented it out.

Unfortunately, Doug only had a tourist visa, which meant he wasn't allowed to work in the UK. He ended up being deported to the US, for which he did have a work visa, as he was planning to marry an American woman.

Despite some aspects of the business not being well organised, revenue continued to grow and it wasn't long before we had forty people working for us, most on a casual basis. We had sales teams of four: three people to generate leads and one to close the deal. We recruited a lot of students, who fitted shifts around their studies. People were coming and going all the time. Basically, we employed anyone who could talk. We paid a weekly wage of £150 plus a commission of £15 per contract. If someone was good at their job, they could make reasonable money.

One day, however, I received a letter from HMRC saying someone who had worked for us had alleged that we weren't paying the minimum hourly wage. This was true, but staff could earn good commission, which could take them well above the minimum wage rate. HMRC carried out an investigation and told us that we couldn't include commission in our hourly rate. Having no choice but to comply, we changed our pay structures.

Even though our sales were going up, our income fluctuated, and occasionally I had to use my credit cards to help pay the staff. Some months it was touch-and-go. The company took a major step forward when we started working through Online Direct, an energy broker that used sub-brokers. That was what we effectively became, and it made our jobs a good deal easier. Online Direct had a deal with Shell Gas, who would obtain bank details from the customer once supply went live, and didn't require credit checks. That really lightened the workload for us.

As sometimes happens when two people set up a business, Gavin and I didn't always agree on how the company should be run, and we had a number of arguments. I could see he wasn't happy. It's good to have a partner in business, as it means you share the worries. The downside is that you need the authority of the other person to make any changes, and you can have major differences of opinion. It came as no surprise when Gavin arrived in the office one morning in the summer of 2006 and announced he was quitting.

'I'm sorry, James, but I want to go travelling,' he said.

'No problem, mate. I completely understand.'

'I mean, I still think this is a good business, but I just want to do other things at the moment.'

'Don't worry, there are no hard feelings, Gav. You've got to do what you feel is right.'

'You sure?'

'Yeah, I'll just carry on.'

It would be strange not having Gavin as a business partner. He was the one who had brought me into the energy business. It was he who had taken the staff out for a drink on Fridays for team-building, while I was taxi-driving. So he would leave a big hole. But I felt confident that, with Sally's support, I could continue to grow the company.

9

CLAWBACKS AND OTHER TROUBLES

WITH GAVIN GONE, I DECIDED to scale back the business. We moved to the lower floor of Fernie House, which was smaller, so the rent was cheaper. The main reason I scaled back was because I wasn't sure if I wanted to stay in the energy business; it wasn't a particularly interesting industry to work in.

I let most of the people working for us go, leaving just Sally and me and half a dozen sales staff, including Sally's fifteen-year-old daughter. I made all the sales calls and the others generated leads, while Sally took care of all the admin. Sally also became a director.

Another reason I scaled down was because we'd had a lot of clawbacks: cases where we'd been paid commissions on sites that didn't go live, or on deals where there were complaints. The best way of looking at our commissions was an interest-free loan; if the customer never used the service, the supplier would call the money back. It was a system which created the illusion that we were doing better than we were.

If we weren't careful, it could cause havoc with our finances.

Downsizing the business led to sales dropping by around 80 per cent, but I had expected this. On the upside, managing a much smaller team was less stressful, so a drop in revenue was a price worth paying.

We were now also working with Opus Energy and Total Direct, although most of our contracts were with Shell Gas through Online Direct. I was getting to know lots of people in the industry. Sally and I were invited to an Npower energy conference in London, with a wine-tasting and a dinner. This was the first time I'd been to a supplier event. We made a weekend of it and went to see the musical *Footloose* in the West End. Mostly, however, with running the taxis and Business Energy Consultants, I was working eighty or ninety hours a week. I often thought about Paul Johnson and his set-up. He lived in a lovely house at Congleton in Cheshire and worked from home. He didn't have all the hassles that go with taxi driving and managing staff, or the pressures involved in trying to grow a business. There were times when I wondered if I should do the same as Gavin and quit the energy business to do something else.

Since we launched the company, our recruitment had been done by word-of-mouth. For example, I might mention to someone in a pub that we were looking for sales staff. That's how Andy Brooks joined us. Andy was a colourful character who was well known around Market Harborough. I knew his personal life was a bit chaotic, but he had the gift of the gab and I thought he would be perfect at closing deals on the phone, so I offered him a job on our sales team. He turned out to be brilliant and was soon closing a couple of deals a day. He was one of the people I kept on when we slimmed down.

Andy was a big Arsenal fan. If Arsenal lost on a Sunday,

he wouldn't come to work on Monday. On one occasion, he invited me and Friz to go with him to see Arsenal play Liverpool at the Emirates Stadium. I'm not that interested in watching matches that don't involve Leicester City, but I thought it would be a good day out. The kick off wasn't until 4pm, so we'd have plenty of time to go drinking beforehand.

We took the train to London on the Sunday morning. During the journey, we drank cans of lager and chatted about football and business. Friz's company, Imperial Corporate Events, was continuing to grow and was expanding its range of corporate events.

As soon as we arrived at St Pancras, we headed to the nearest pub. After a few drinks we took the Piccadilly Line to Finsbury Park, where we went to a couple more pubs. By the time we got to the ground, we were all the worse for wear, so much so that I can't remember anything about the game.

Obviously, the sensible thing to have done after the match would have been to take the train back to Market Harborough. But we didn't do that. We did the stupid thing and carried on drinking, having decided to catch the 10.30pm train. In one pub, Friz returned from the bar with a tray of Aftershocks, which we all downed straight away.

We arrived at St Pancras at just after ten. What happened next is a blur, but I can remember a large Asian guy on the concourse who kept staring at me. He was with a woman. The next thing, he ran towards me, knocking me to the floor, and jumped on me. He began furiously punching me. I tried to cover my face with my hands. Friz had already left us by this point, but Andy came to my aid and eventually he dragged the guy off me. Several station staff appeared and told us they had called the police. We wouldn't be allowed to board our trains until they came.

When the police arrived, they arrested Andy, me and our attacker. He was put in the back of one police van, and Andy and I in the back of another. I can remember sitting in the back of the police van making silly jokes about Robin Hood and the Sheriff of Nottingham, because the surname of the officer who'd arrested me was Nottingham.

We were taken to a nearby police station, where I spent the night in a cell. When I woke up the next morning, I felt dreadful. I tried to remember what had happened; I couldn't work out why the guy had attacked me. I phoned Sally to tell her I was okay and to briefly explain what had happened. I told her not to worry, as it would all be sorted out.

Later that morning, I met the duty solicitor, who advised me to say I'd just had a few too many drinks. I was escorted into a room and interviewed by three senior detectives who, for some reason, had come from another police station. I was told that the guy had accused me of making racist comments.

'No comment,' I said.

'Why did you attack him?' asked one of the detectives.

'No comment.'

'Do you realise the seriousness of this?' asked another detective.

'What do you mean?'

'You were convicted of racially aggravated assault in 2003.'

'Yeah, but I didn't do anything wrong at the station. He attacked me.'

'Okay, so tell us what you say happened.'

I explained as best I could what I could remember about the incident and answered the questions that were put to me.

The duty solicitor asked the officers to pause the interview, as he wanted to speak to me in private. They said that was fine and stepped outside.

'Listen, it looks like the fact that you were drunk hasn't been logged,' said the duty solicitor.

'Yeah, I was surprised they didn't ask me about this,' I said.

'So, don't mention it. Just say you remember everything and you didn't do anything wrong.'

At the end of the interview, I was told I was being released pending further enquiries. When I asked when Andy would be released, one of the detectives said there had been a warrant out for him and he would be appearing at a magistrates' court somewhere in London on Tuesday morning for unpaid fines. He added that he had been put on bail for £1,500, but Andy had said he couldn't afford to pay it. I said I would. After leaving the police station at around 3pm, I went to a cashpoint and withdrew the money, then returned to the police station. Andy was released.

On the train back to Market Harborough, I was worried sick. What should have been a fun day out in London had ended with me facing possible charges, not just of violence but with a racial component. But this time I was certain I was entirely the victim of what had happened. I replayed the incident in my mind, but I still couldn't recall saying anything racist to the guy. Nevertheless, if this was pinned on me, I could be looking at a couple of years in prison. I remembered Phil, the guy at North Sea Camp who had been given an eighteen-month sentence for racially aggravated harassment after sending anti-semitic emails and text messages. I'd worked hard to rebuild my life after coming out of prison. Business Energy Consultants was doing well. If I was sent down again, that would most likely be the end of my role in the business. This time, I might end up in a harsher prison than North Sea Camp. And now I had so much more to lose.

If the worry of facing charges of a racist assault and possibly ending up in prison again wasn't bad enough, things were not going well at Spotty Dog. I'd reached the point where I just couldn't continue to run both Business Energy Consultants and a taxi business.

I had come to hate running taxis. It was incredibly hard work and you had no social life. One of my problems was that, as ever, I couldn't turn a job down. If someone phoned for a taxi and there wasn't a driver available, I'd pick them up in my car, just as I had done in the early days when I started the firm. And as ever, I was often so tired that I'd find myself falling asleep at the wheel and have to pull over. I'd set my alarm and sleep for a few minutes and then carry on driving. If I was working late at night, I'd drink multiple cups of coffee to keep me awake. It was crazy. And it wasn't as if I was making much cash. At times I'd queue on the rank for an hour and then when I got to the front a customer would turn up and ask me to take them around the corner, and I'd only earn two pounds fifty. It was heart-breaking.

Along the way, tensions between Tom and me had also started to grow, as I didn't feel he was as committed as me. If he was having a break and a customer phoned, or if someone asked for a car at half-five in the morning, he'd turn the job down. This led to arguments between us. We even ended up having a drunken fight one time about who was going to do a particularly early morning job to Heathrow. It's probably true to say that I was more passionate about the business than Tom. But perhaps he was more realistic, not letting it rule his life.

Another time, Tom and I went to pick up an eight-seater Citroën minibus in Watford. We were heading down the M1, with me driving and Tom in the passenger seat. There were roadworks and, somehow, I ended up smashing into the back of a Volvo. I was unhurt, as was the driver of the Volvo, but

Tom was taken to Luton Hospital by ambulance. The police turned up and closed the M1 for forty-five minutes. After our car had been towed away, I continued the journey to Watford by taxi. On the way back, I collected Tom from the hospital. He was wearing a neck brace, but other than that, thankfully, he was fine.

I had to appear in court for driving without due care and attention. The magistrate gave me six points on my licence and fined me £200. He also sent me on a two-day drivers' rehabilitation course in Northampton, which involved sitting in a classroom and then going out with an instructor, who had to pass you as fit to drive. I couldn't wait for it to end. It reminded me of community service.

All this meant that Tom wanted to get out of the taxi game and do something else. When I suggested that we sell Spotty Dog, he readily agreed. We started putting out feelers for a potential buyer.

Back at the energy business, my anxiety over the possible repercussions of what had happened at St Pancras Station made it hard to concentrate at work. I tried to put it out of my mind, but I couldn't. I'd find myself thinking back to the day I was sentenced at Leicester Crown Court and then taken down to the cell to wait for the prison van. The most important part of my day had now become the postman's delivery each morning to our house in Middlebrook Green. Over the following weeks, I waited anxiously to hear from the police. I'd phone Sally in the mornings and ask her to check any letters that had arrived for me.

She phoned one lunchtime and said there was a letter from the police.

'Go on, what does it say?' I said, my heart pumping.

'It says they aren't taking any further action.'

'Are you a hundred per cent sure?'

'Yeah.'

'Can you read it to me?'

As Sally slowly read the letter, I listened intently. It was true. They weren't taking any action. After putting the phone down, relief surged through me.

I also felt huge relief when Tom and I managed to sell Spotty Dog to Barry Bradley, who had once owned Murphy's, for £50,000. We did the deal in a pub. By the time we'd paid all our debts, we were only left with about £10,000 each, but we had got rid of the burden that the firm had become. After Barry retired to Spain, his son Jody took over the company. Unfortunately, it later went bankrupt.

Although Business Energy Consultants was ticking over, things hadn't been quite the same since Gavin had left, and I still wasn't sure if energy switching was really the business for me. So I began to look for other business ideas to get involved in. I'd heard that Dubai was becoming popular with Westerners and that there were opportunities in its property market. When I discovered a company called Your Dubai Home, a website for people looking to buy property in the city, I bought it.

I needed to see what Dubai was actually like and talk to people in the property market there, so I booked tickets for Sally and me and we flew out. We stayed in a cheap hotel in a district called Karama, near the fish market. I'd never been anywhere so hot; the heat on the streets was overwhelming. We hired a driver to take us around the city. He took us to the Atlantis Hotel, which was about to open, Palm Island and other places of interest. There were skyscrapers everywhere, glitzy shopping centres, and the roads were wide and modern.

I had several meetings with various property people and went to some events. One of the investors I met was, apparently, very well connected in Pakistan. I put down deposits on two villas off-plan, seeing them as excellent investments.

I came away from Dubai thinking it wasn't a place I'd particularly want to visit again. Sally felt the same. While it was an interesting city in many respects, it didn't seem to have any soul. As it happened, the villas on which I'd put deposits never got built because of the financial crash in 2008, so I lost all my money.

We had another trip abroad when Doug, with whom I'd kept in touch, invited Sally and me to his wedding in a small town in Ohio. We spent a few days there, staying in a cheap motel. The night before the wedding, I joined Doug and some of his ice-hockey mates for the stag night. We all got drunk and ended up in a strip club. Sally and I had to rely on Doug to pick us up each day. During our trip, I probably put on a stone, as we ate at Wendy's all the time.

While I was there, I received a phone call from a reporter on the *Daily Telegraph*. He said he'd been contacted by the owner of a fish-and-chip shop in Hampshire who claimed that one of our sales team had signed him up – without his knowledge – for a three-year gas contract with Shell. He'd contacted Shell about this but hadn't got anywhere. I told the reporter that I'd check our phone records when I returned to the UK.

This kind of complaint wasn't unusual. Customers often complained about contracts. Some were trying to get out of them, or they'd been contacted by other energy brokers offering better deals. As soon as I returned to Market Harborough, I investigated the issue and couldn't find the fish-and-chip shop owner's details in our BT records. It looked like one of our team might have been guilty of mis-selling. I spoke to Shell, who released the customer from the contract.

Around this time, I re-established contact with my daughter

Hannah, who was now thirteen. I hadn't seen her for six years. I should have done more to maintain the contact, but with everything that was going on, I gave up. Now I found her on Facebook and sent her a friend request, wondering if she'd remember me. She replied, telling me she had left Devon and was living with her granny in a village called Bourne, near Stamford in Lincolnshire. Charlotte had also moved nearby. A little later, I arranged to pick Hannah up and we went to a garden centre for the afternoon. Her granny came along, but things went fine. After that, I started seeing Hannah regularly. I'd pick her up in Bourne, spend the day with her and then take her back in the evening. Eventually, her granny allowed her to stay over and then spend the weekends with me.

Despite my ambivalence about working in the industry, Business Energy Consultants was growing again. We started working with Npower and when Economy Power was sold to Eon Energy, this gave us our first big customer. Eon supplied around 700,000 business customers through its Powergen and Eon Energy brands, together with around 8.1 million residential customer accounts. Rediscovering my optimism, I was much more settled and beginning to feel that anything was possible for the company.

What I could not have foreseen was that one of my most important business relationships was about to be rekindled and another was to unexpectedly end.

10

A NEW VENTURE

ONE DAY IN APRIL 2009, out of the blue, Gavin phoned me. I hadn't heard from him in ages. All I knew was that he was involved in selling mortgages.

'So how's Business Energy Consultants?' he asked cheerily.

'Doing well, mate.'

'Listen, I've got an idea for you.'

'Go on.'

'To set up a reverse auction energy website.'

'I thought you were done with the energy business, Gav.'

'I was. But I can see this making a lot of money.'

He explained that the site would enable customers to see the prices of all the energy suppliers. When someone's contract ended, suppliers would place a bid for it. The lowest price would win, and we would get a commission.

'Yeah, it sounds interesting,' I said.

'How about investing in it, then?'

'Let's meet up and talk about it.'

We met in the Angel a couple of days later, and Gavin talked more about his business idea, telling me he wanted to bring in a guy called James Livermore, who had been his manager at Carrington Carr, the mortgage and insurance company he'd worked for. Gavin reckoned James was brilliant at sales and training staff. He'd had the clever idea of contacting the people to whom he'd sold Payment Protection Insurance (PPI) and handling any claims for compensation they had. I didn't need much convincing. Gavin's proposal struck me as a sound one, and I was in.

He proposed to name the new company Utility Bidder, and I was to make the bulk of the investment. The plan was that Gavin, James and I would each own 33 per cent. Because Gavin had a bad credit rating, he didn't put his name down as a director; he planned to do this later. So James and I became fifty-fifty shareholders until then. It was all agreed on a handshake. Gavin also brought in Richard Thorpe, another colleague from Carrington Carr, to join the sales team.

Utility Bidder took the upper floor of Fernie House, so I was now involved in two energy-switching companies operating out of the same building. As time went on, this caused friction and arguments over leads between the sales teams of Business Energy Consultants and the new company. We were doing exactly the same work, and naturally there was a certain amount of rivalry between the two companies. But I saw them as two teams, not two separate companies. There was so much business to go after that it didn't matter that we were two different firms. Gavin and I never saw ourselves as rivals, and we would meet each day to discuss various issues.

Unlike Gavin, I was spending a lot of time each day on the phone. I tried to bring in £30,000 revenue a month for Business

Energy Consultants, often working until late. Since the rest of the staff were earning their own keep with the contracts they sold themselves, all the money I was bringing in went to the company. Gavin had to virtually beg me to come off the phones. One of the sales I did was with a glass manufacturer that spent over £1 million on energy each year. Looking back, though, I might have been better spending more time training staff, as Gavin had suggested.

Paul Johnson had started a brokerage business called Direct Energy Associates and he got us involved with British Gas. I'd negotiated a deal with Paul which meant he earned 10 per cent commission on £100,000 of sales. We were soon making him a lot of money. I had a good relationship with Paul and would meet with him quite often, even going to his fiftieth birthday party at his house in Cheshire.

If we knew when contracts were due to end, we'd know when British Gas would send a renewal letter. The sales team would phone a customer around the time it was due and say, 'Look out for the letter.' If a customer produced the letter, we could offer a better price. It was almost like a game of poker and knowing what cards the other player held.

Paul arranged a meeting at our offices with Jag, an account manager for British Gas in Leicester. He seemed to be a smart guy, and I kept in touch with him, inviting him to play golf one weekend. Over a few beers in the clubhouse afterwards, I said to him that we needed to deal directly with British Gas. This was the best option for the business: we would save £10,000 a month, which would give us £120,000 extra annual profit. Jag said he would try to arrange this, but I'd have to tell Paul Johnson that I'd approached British Gas.

I phoned Paul and invited him out to lunch at a pub near his house. Driving up the A50 to Congleton, I rehearsed in my mind what I would say to him. It wasn't a meeting I was looking forward to, but it had to be done.

'Sounds like the business is doing well, James,' said Paul as we sat down.

'Yeah, we're getting busier all the time,' I said.

'Energy switching's a fast-growing market, isn't it?'

'Listen, Paul, there's something I wanted to talk to you about.'

'Fire away. What is it?'

'I want to deal directly with British Gas.'

'What? Are you serious?'

'Yeah.'

Paul was silent for a moment and then said angrily, 'What you're really saying is you want to cut me out!'

'Listen, Paul, I have to think about the financial success of the company.'

'But you're cutting me out.' He jabbed his finger at me. 'That's it, isn't it?'

'It's just that it makes more sense for us to deal directly with British Gas.'

'And I lose money.'

'Look, we've had a good working relationship, but this is something we have to do.'

'I hadn't expected this,' he said, shaking his head. 'You know what, James?'

'What?'

He narrowed his eyes. 'It feels like you're screwing me over.'

'Look, things change, Paul. I'm sorry.'

I could understand his reaction. If Business Energy Consultants dealt with British Gas directly, he would lose several thousand pounds a month. I think he'd bought a chalet in a ski resort in France and was relying on income from

Business Energy Consultants to pay for it. If I'd been him, I would probably have felt the same. After that meeting, he cut me off, owing us several thousand pounds in commission. I was sorry about the way things had ended, but I had to think about what was best for the company. In business you sometimes have to make tough decisions, and this was one of them. It was made tougher because I genuinely liked Paul, and he'd been such an important figure for me in the energy business.

Back in the East Midlands, unemployment was high and the Job Centre used to send jobless people to us for trials. They would all still receive their social security benefits, plus expenses for lunch and travel.

When we had ten people come for a trial, I had the idea to do our own version of the TV show *The Apprentice*. James and I took on the roles of Alan Sugar and Karen Brady. I split the group into two teams and gave them the task of going out to businesses in Market Harborough to try to get the owners to give them letters of authority. A letter of authority would allow us to access the energy account of a customer and find out how much energy they used, the cost of it and when the contract ended. I told the group that at the end of the task, three of them would be offered jobs and the other seven would be let go. This wasn't true; we would take all of them on if they were good enough. Before they were sent out, we provided them with training.

The winning team went to the pub and the losers were brought back into the boardroom. We asked them why they had lost the task and which members of the team were the weakest. They then had to decide who should be fired. There were a few tears, but these soon dried up when I told them that we were offering everyone jobs. We all went to the pub to celebrate.

The new recruits trained on the job by sitting next to experienced members of staff. We'd give them copies of the *Yellow Pages* and tell them to ring businesses and ask them if they would like to save money on their energy bills. If someone said yes, and most people did, they would be passed to a more experienced member of the team.

Gavin, James and I discussed setting up our own energy supply company, which meant we'd be able to sell gas ourselves. But, in the end, we decided against it. It was probably good that we did, as many small energy suppliers went bust later on.

Up to that point, I'd been using the bookkeeper I'd taken on when I was running Spotty Dog. But I now felt I needed someone with more financial experience and knowledge, so I hired Cheyettes, a local accountancy company.

Andy was still working for me, but he and Gavin didn't get on, and arguments often broke out between them. To try to keep the peace, I'd sit both of them down and try to defuse the situation. It didn't create the right atmosphere in the office if people were having blazing rows. When I left the building, I would worry that it would all kick off between Andy and Gavin while I was out.

I was aware that Andy was dealing with a number of personal issues, and his wife had moved to Australia with his child. He'd sometimes disappear for days. On one occasion, I let him use the company credit card, and he racked up several thousand pounds.

Perhaps unwisely, I allowed the staff to have a drink in the office on Friday afternoons if we'd had a good week of sales. One day, Andy picked up a pint glass, smashed it on a desk and lunged at Gavin with it.

'What the fuck do you think you're doing?' I shouted,

springing up and snatching the glass out of Andy's hand.

'That cunt's always winding me up,' he screamed, pointing at Gavin.

'Piss off!' yelled Gavin, visibly shaken. 'James, get him the fuck out!'

I took Andy by the arm and led him into the boardroom and sat him down. Once he'd calmed down, I said, 'Look, mate, I'm really sorry, but I can't have this sort of stuff going on.'

'I know. I don't know what came over me,' he murmured.

'That was bloody stupid. You could have seriously injured Gav.'

'I just got angry with him.'

'Andy, I don't want to do this, but I'm going to have to let you go.'

He didn't argue. He knew he'd overstepped the mark. I didn't want to sack him, because he'd been a brilliant sales agent, but I didn't feel I had any alternative. Years later, Andy admitted to me that he'd lost one of the biggest opportunities he'd ever had.

Gavin had a few mates who had gone out to Thailand and were interested in earning some money. So he recruited them for the Utility Bidder sales team. He flew to Thailand to meet a guy about building a website, or auction platform, and database for Utility Bidder. One morning, he was riding a motorbike and had to swerve to avoid a truck coming towards him, causing him to smash into a woman on another motor-bike. The woman's nephew was a senior police officer, who confiscated Gavin's passport and demanded a sum of money to return it. I had to go and see Gavin's dad to explain what had happened. He paid the money and Gavin got his passport back.

The idea of building an online auction platform never

happened, for one reason or another; basically, Utility Bidder ended up doing much the same as Business Energy Consultants. But once Gavin was safely back in the UK, he and I agreed that both companies needed to become more professional. We launched websites for Business Energy Consultants and Utility Bidder and started to contact customers by email as well as by phone. Communicating by email slowed things down at the beginning, as the sales team only wanted to sell on the phone; it was what they were used to. But if you want to be a successful business, you have to move with the times. You can't afford to get stuck in a rut.

We were definitely behind the times when it came to technology. We still recorded everything on paper and we didn't have a database. We relied on Sally's filing system for information about customers and suppliers. Although we had computers, we only used them to record phone calls. We had no database or CRM (Customer Relations Management) system, so we poached Jake from the IT company next door and made him head of IT. He built a CRM for us.

As Gavin and I were now well-established in the energy business, we started expanding into other sectors where a lot of energy was used. We targeted hotels, care homes, private schools, academies, colleges, sports clubs and spas. The more energy a company used, of course, the more we got paid. We didn't target large organisations like the NHS, as it would mean bidding for the energy contracts, which would be complicated and incredibly time-consuming. To get those contracts meant jumping through a lot of hoops.

As a marketing initiative, we ran a competition offering free energy for a year. Companies had to sign up within three months and then they'd go into the draw. In a great stroke of luck for us, a florist – whose annual energy bill was only six or seven hundred pounds – won the contest.

Most of the people who ran restaurants and takeaways were Indian, Chinese or Turkish and didn't speak English that well. That meant they didn't understand their energy bills. I would go to Chinatown in London and walk around and try to meet the owners of some of the restaurants. Chinese restaurants use an incredible amount of gas. It was difficult, though, to get restaurants to sign up.

One of my first customers was Desmond Tang. Chinese restaurants change hands often, and some owners disappear owing money to energy suppliers. Because of this, energy suppliers usually ask for a security deposit before taking someone on. Desmond wouldn't pay the £1,500 British Gas was asking for, so I paid it, as the deal was worth £5,000 to Utility Bidder.

I became quite friendly with Desmond. If I went to London for a football match or to go to a show with Sally, I'd often pop in to see him. He'd always tell me to sit down and order what I wanted off the menu, and he'd open a bottle of champagne. He also referred Utility Bidder to other restaurants.

One time, I went to Desmond's restaurant with two friends. Desmond gave me £2,000 in cash he owed me for some consultancy work, and I stuffed it into my jacket pocket. After we left, we spent the rest of the day drinking in the pubs in Soho before taking the train back to Corby later in the evening. For some treason, we got off the train at Kettering and went to a nightclub. I ended up dancing with my shirt off, so the bouncers ejected me. I can't remember where I went, but I remember coming around at about two in the morning on a bench and realising I didn't have my jacket, which had two grand and my phone in it. I returned to the nightclub and told one of the bouncers I'd left my jacket. He went inside and came back with it.

'You know, mate, you've got two grand in one of the pockets.'

'Yeah, I know,' I said.

'I found your mum's number on your phone and called her to tell her about the money,' he said.

I thanked him. I don't think many bouncers would be so honest. I should have given him a reward, but because I was so out of it, it never occurred to me.

One day, Desmond phoned me and said he had a problem with his gas supply. I phoned a gas engineer and asked him to visit the restaurant and fix it. A couple of hours later he phoned me to say that Desmond was stealing gas and the supply to his restaurant was unsafe. British Gas had a special team dedicated to catching people who stole gas. I phoned Desmond and told him he couldn't do this.

I'd also been trying to get the nearby Chinese restaurant Gerrard's Corner to sign up with us, as I knew it was out of contract and had been paying far too much for its gas. But each time I called there I never managed to speak to the owner. The staff either wouldn't tell me who he was or they pretended they didn't speak English. After being given the runaround yet again, I improvised in a way that I was confident would get the owner's attention. I won't go into every detail, but it involved a communication from myself to Shell which I was almost certain would lead to a call between Shell and the owner.

Sure enough, Shell phoned the owner and ended up giving him my mobile number.

'What's going on?' the owner said when he called me.

'By going with Shell, you'll save £30,000 a year,' I said. 'I've been trying to contact you to tell you this. It's a brilliant deal for you.'

'Thirty thousand? That much?' he said.

'Yes!'

'Okay, well, in that case, I'm very happy.'

We also hired some guys at a call centre in India to go through the Transco database looking for companies that used a lot of energy. They'd do fifty searches an hour for two pounds. Their job was to get leads and then arrange a callback from one of the sales agents. Often, when one of the team called back, they'd be told by the customer that they hadn't requested a callback. The staff at the Indian call centre weren't particularly good and their accents were a problem for customers. But they did produce one good lead – with a vicar who was involved in running the Northumberland Church of England Academy Trust. Through him, I signed up seven schools. The timing was right. The schools had just come out of contract with their supplier.

Gavin and I had a falling-out when he claimed I'd made £1 million from Online Direct and hadn't told him about it. Sally and I had been on holiday in Spain, and Gavin had agreed to pick us up at East Midlands Airport. But before we left Spain, he phoned to say he wouldn't be collecting us and that he wanted a meeting with me.

When Gavin and I met in the Angel in Market Harborough, I could see that he'd worked himself up because I'd been away and he hadn't been able to talk to me about the money he thought I'd made. I told him I hadn't made a million. We didn't speak for a few weeks, but eventually he accepted that I was telling the truth.

But pilfering did happen. On one occasion, a member of the team brought his own PC in and stole data because he was planning to start up his own energy brokerage. I put some software onto the computer he was using and saw that he was taking data. I had no choice but to sack him.

Unfortunately, things were not working out with James Livermore, our co-owner. He was a real people person and was good at talking to staff and helping them if they had any problems. He was probably more understanding than Gavin and I would have been. However, Gavin and I felt he wasn't spending enough time at the office, and this resulted in arguments. Gavin and James had several blazing rows in front of the staff, and I had to tell them to go elsewhere if they wanted to argue.

James knew his days at Utility Bidder were numbered. Just before Christmas in 2013, he asked me if I wanted to buy his shares. I agreed and paid him £350,000 in the name of Corporate Images, of which Sally was a director. I gave her 40 per cent of the shares. This upset Gavin, as he was now a minority shareholder, which devalued his shares. He said he'd sell me his shares for £500,000, but I refused.

A couple of years earlier, flying back from a trip to Spain, I saw an advert in the in-flight magazine for the Barbados British Airways Football Legends Tournament, which was taking place in June 2011. Alan Shearer, Teddy Sheringham, Andy Cole, Dwight Yorke, Darren Anderton and other former players were taking part. I thought it sounded fun, so I decided to go with Sally. I booked flights with Virgin and accommodation at Almond Beach Club in St Lawrence Gap, knowing nothing about Barbados.

We boarded the 747 at Heathrow, took our seats in the middle of the plane and settled back for the eight-and-a-half-hour flight. A couple of hours after we'd taken off, I heard a commotion behind us. People were shouting and screaming. I craned my neck over the seat, but I couldn't work out what was happening.

The captain made an announcement. 'This is an absolute

disgrace. If we could divert, we would. No one is to move and everyone must put on their seatbelts for the rest of the flight. No alcohol will be served. If you want to use the toilet, you must press the button.'

While I was waiting to use the toilet, another passenger told me there had been a fight and the cabin crew had broken it up. He said a group of about ten people at the back of the plane were quite drunk and rowdy, and a few kids had been running up and down the aisle. One little boy had started being sick and his dad had tried to grab him, accidentally knocking into a couple of the drunk guys. One of them was livid and put the dad in a headlock while his mate jumped in and started punching him in the face. But the dad fought back and ended up knocking the guy out cold.

When the plane landed in Barbados, police boarded the plane and arrested three passengers.

We took the transfer to the hotel. As we were checking in, Dwight Yorke walked past, then Alan Shearer and then Teddy Sheringham. They were all staying at our hotel. I felt so excited.

I went to the bar; a lot of the players were there drinking. I took photos and got chatting to some of them, but I didn't talk much about football, as I would probably have asked them the same things everybody else asks them. I talked more about golf because I knew a lot of them were golfers. I'd taken the game up the previous year and played regularly with Jag.

I recognised a bald guy as Rob Beasley from Sky Sport's *Sunday Supplement* football chat show. I told him about what had happened on the plane. He asked if he could have my mobile number. The next morning, my phone went mental, with journalists wanting to interview me about the incident. I sold the story to *The Sun* and *The Mirror*.

The tournament was six-a-side and was to be held at the

Kensington Oval. One of its aims was to raise money for local charities involved in the development of football in the Caribbean.

On the morning of the tournament, I got talking to former Arsenal and Liverpool player Jimmy Carter, who was playing for Liverpool Legends.

'We're short,' he said.

'I'll play,' I said, and explained that I'd played lots of football and even had trials for Leicester City and Scunthorpe United.

'We could put you on the bench.'

'Yeah, that would be great.' I could see my big moment coming up, a chance to play with players who had been some of the best in the world.

He went to ask the guy in charge of the team, but, sadly, he said no.

At the after-party, I got chatting to Gary Speed, the former Welsh international and Wales manager. I made the mistake of asking him what he thought England's chances were in the European Championships.

'England?' he said.

'Yeah, what do you reckon?' I said.

'I don't give a fuck about England!'

And that was the end of the conversation.

I'm someone who enjoys new challenges, and I like to push myself to see how far I can go. I was working long hours at Business Energy Consultants, but I felt I needed to do something else as well.

One day in 2013, a noticed an advert on Facebook looking for people to take part in a boxing contest. It was aimed at novices who had never boxed before. I'd watched a Sky TV documentary about Freddy Flintoff learning to box under the guidance of Barry McGuigan and his son, and I'd found it intriguing. The contest in the advert was being organised by Ultra White Collar Boxing. You had to commit to eight weeks' training and raise some money for Cancer Research UK. At the end of the training, you would take part in a boxing match of three two-minute rounds at a nightclub called the Republic in Leicester. The man behind Ultra White Collar Boxing was Jon Leonard, who ran a gym in Derby.

The only boxing I'd ever done – apart from in the cloakroom at Welland Park College – was in the RAF, when I'd been punched so hard during a sparring session that I never went back in the ring. But I'd had a fascination with the sport ever since seeing Sylvester Stallone in the *Rocky* films.

I was in two minds whether to sign up. Part of me thought it would be exciting and a way of getting fit, but part of me thought it could be dangerous – and I didn't want to end up in hospital.

Then Buzz came to see me in the office one day, and I mentioned that I was thinking of taking up boxing, but I was in two minds about it.

'You serious?' he said.

'Like I say, I don't know,' I said.

'Go for it, James.'

'You reckon?'

'Dead right. I'll come and watch you fight.'

And like that, I signed up.

11

IN AND OUT OF THE RING

FOLLOWING AN INITIAL Ultra White Collar Boxing meeting in Leicester, I started training three times a week: one evening at a fitness class at the Republic, where you would use punch bags, and two evenings at a gym. I became obsessed with training and started doing extra sessions. I'd do weights in the morning at the gym and then box on the Monday evening at the Republic and at boxing gyms on other evenings.

To take part in the event, you had to agree to raise at least fifty pounds for Cancer Research UK. I raised money through several raffles at Business Energy Consultants and Utility Bidder. I sold over a hundred tickets for the fight to family, friends and staff. The prospect of getting into the ring in front of a crowd had now started to become real.

After the eight weeks' training, you were matched up with someone of similar ability. I was disappointed to learn that I'd been paired with Scott Jones, as he was much smaller than me. I am six-foot-three and I weighed thirteen stone. In some ways it felt like a bit of an insult. I'd sparred with Scott and he didn't seem that special, so I felt very confident. On the other hand, I reminded myself, he could have just taken it easy when sparring, and he might turn out to be pretty good when it came to the fight.

A fight in a pub is usually over in seconds. But these fights were planned. In a pub you could get glassed or kicked in the head, whereas in a boxing ring you had protection – although it was no guarantee that you wouldn't get injured.

I arrived at the Republic on the day of the fight at about 1pm, feeling a mixture of fear and excitement. I was going to box in front of my family, friends and colleagues, but I could end up getting seriously injured. The first thing I had to do was have a medical. Thankfully, I passed. I discovered I would be fighting last. All the fighters had to wait in a glass VIP lounge overlooking the ring. The club quickly filled up and the crowd was buzzing with anticipation. My dad and Sally were somewhere in there. The first fight started at around five o'clock. Each one consisted of three two-minute rounds, with the referee deciding the winner (if both contestants were still on their feet by the end). Watching the fighters battle it out, I couldn't wait for the moment when I would climb into the ring. While I waited, I received lots of text messages from friends saying things like, 'Go and smash him up.'

My fight didn't happen until about half-past-nine, by which time I felt pumped up and raring to go. I had chosen 'James Lights Out Longley' as my ring name, which was emblazoned on the back of my red vest. Wearing a head guard, mouth guard and other protective gear, I made my way through the crowd towards the ring to the sound of 'Here I Go Again' by Whitesnake, one of my favourite songs, and climbed into the ring. The atmosphere was electric, with people shouting and cheering. I'd experienced some brilliant atmospheres at Leicester City games, but nothing compared to this. At a football match I was a spectator, but now I was centre-stage. What I was feeling must be similar to what footballers experience when they emerge from the tunnel for a big game. I fully admit I loved being the centre of this attention. It gave me a real buzz. I was desperate to win and I felt confident that I would, given all the extra training I'd done.

Once the bell rang, I didn't hear the roar of the crowd, because I was so focused on how to land punches on my opponent and avoid being hit by him. It was scary, but at the same time I had a huge adrenaline rush. I'd seen lots of fights where people had been out after one round because they tried to knock their opponent out. I reasoned that if my breathing was good when I sat down after the first round, then I'd get stronger in the second and third rounds. Sure enough, I won the fight.

When I stepped out of the ring, I was shattered. I realised just how much stamina it must take to fight twelve rounds. But I was on an incredible high. The highs I'd experienced after winning a football match didn't come close to this.

Then came the comedown. For the first few days after the fight, I felt depressed. After psyching myself up for weeks, it was all over. I missed the focus the fight had given me. Talking to others who had boxed, they said they'd had similar feelings.

The obvious solution was to sign up for a second event. I persuaded twelve guys from Harborough to train for fights against twelve guys from Leicester, again at the Republic. I arranged for a gym in Harborough to train us.

In my first fight, I'd felt comfortable and confident that I'd win. The second one was different. The lad I was matched with sent me text messages saying he was going to put me in Leicester Royal Infirmary. Part of this was just banter, but I think it was partly also serious. However, for some reason he didn't turn up. A guy who had already boxed that evening volunteered to fight again. I won, but it was a hollow victory because I didn't feel it was right for the guy to be fighting twice in one evening.

I boxed a third time, at Pride Park in Derby, where I'd booked one of the conference rooms for the Business Energy Consultants and Utility Bidder staff Christmas party. I invited a number of suppliers, including Jag from British Gas. I only decided at the last minute to fight, so I hadn't done the usual eight weeks' training, but I'd been to Tenerife for ten days and trained in a professional boxing gym there. I came out of the gym in Tenerife one day and my face had swollen up massively after getting caught by a punch in a sparring session that involved three-minute rounds.

I didn't know who I was going to be fighting until I arrived at Pride Park. It turned out I had been matched with a guy who looked to be in great shape. I went on the attack from the start. My opponent had three standing counts, but the referee didn't stop the fight. I completed my third win.

Following the fight, we all went to Fat Cat, a bar in Derby city centre, for the after-party. I was in high spirits. When I sprayed champagne around the room, one of the bouncers ordered me to leave, so we all went to another bar across the street. I can't remember how it happened, but some of my staff ended up getting into a fight. Everyone else rushed outside to get away from the trouble, but I ended up on the floor being kicked by several blokes. I don't know how I escaped without getting seriously injured. Jag was cut on the cheek by a glass, which narrowly missed his eye. By the time the police arrived, the guys who had started the fight had run off.

The incident didn't diminish my enthusiasm for my new sport. After Christmas, I told Jon I'd like to get involved in organising fights. He'd started to expand the business and was raising more money for Cancer Research UK, putting on shows in around fifty locations. He agreed to team up with me and we'd split the profits fifty-fifty. He would arrange the venue, security, referee, ring girls and so on, and Sally and I would do all the promotion, ticket sales and deal with the boxers.

I secured the Kettering Conference Centre as a venue, and we put on a show in April 2014. I matched the fighters, including two people from Utility Bidder who would fight each other, and I trained with some of them. On the night of the fight, one lad failed his medical because of high blood pressure. I had sparred with the lad he was due to fight, so I said I'd step in as a replacement. I had a medical, borrowed some kit and trainers and fought. I won.

I then put on shows in a number of other towns, including Milton Keynes, Bedford and Stevenage. I had to find boxing or MMA gyms to train the fighters, but that wasn't hard, as gyms were always looking for extra income. Some of those who trained at a gym might end up becoming a member or hiring one of its personal trainers.

If you got two hundred people who said they were interested in boxing at one of the shows, a hundred would turn up at the meeting, seventy-five for the training and forty would box. The hardest part of running boxing shows was trying to find replacements when people pulled out a few days beforehand.

The Amateur Boxing Association, as the governing body for boxing in England was then known, hated White Collar Boxing because it didn't conform to its rules. But I thought a lot of ABA boxing shows were boring compared to White

Collar Boxing. You could get anywhere between 500 and 2,000 people turning up for a show – all depending on many boxers were fighting and how many tickets they had sold. The dress code at shows was black tie, which was a way of trying to keep out troublemakers. On occasion, trouble still broke out. At one, two car dealers fought each other. They had both bet ten grand on the fight, but it all kicked off in the crowd and we had to abandon the show. Some venues would pull the plug if fights broke out. Leicester City did this, so we moved to Leicester Tigers rugby club.

People love going to watch their friends box. Sometimes people boxed in memory of a family member or friend who had died. Others might box to try to overcome drink problems or mental health issues. Fighters each had to sell ten tickets and raise at least fifty quid for Cancer Research UK. Ringside tables cost £500, including food; if you didn't want food, it was £350. Standing tickets were twenty pounds. A DJ would play music in the intervals between rounds, and people would get up and dance. The ticket money paid for the event and provided a profit for the organisers. The other money raised went to the cancer charity. As of today, around £30 million has been raised by Ultra White Collar Boxing, which has become one of the largest corporate fundraisers for Cancer Research UK.

I put on fights where there was a big weight difference, and they were good matches. But because of worries over a smaller guy getting injured by a bigger guy, fighters are now matched to within a few pounds of each other. Some people took the boxing more seriously than others and trained harder. In some fights the boxers would just dance around and there'd be nothing going on. But you'd also see some really good fights. Women occasionally boxed at the shows too. The trainers would say the girls always listened when they talked about technique, but the men just wanted to knock each other out.

I loved putting on the boxing shows. Guys who'd fought would come up to me afterwards and say how boxing had changed their lives, perhaps because it had helped them overcome their addiction problems or given them a new purpose in life. Nevertheless, it all eventually became too much for me. The shows were getting bigger, with an increasing focus on health and safety. It was in danger of becoming just another job. At a show I'd put on in Bedford, I'd had to help carry a hundred security barriers up three flights of stairs and then take them back down afterwards. The excitement and enjoyment I'd had at the beginning was no longer there. I was also missing watching Leicester City. When we won 5–3 at home to Man United after being 3–1 down with half an hour to go, I felt gutted that I hadn't been there.

My brother Tom had been helping me run the shows, and gradually he started to manage them. Sometimes I'd just go to a show for a night out, but I was always there if he needed me to help out. In 2015, I told him he could have the business if he fancied being involved full-time. And he did. Like me, he's had his challenges. One night in Luton a massive fight broke out when the political activist Tommy Robinson got in the ring. Bottles and glasses were thrown. It was mayhem.

Running the boxing shows had been a great experience. It was a good period in my life, when everything seemed to click together. But it was time to move on.

12

THE DIRECTORS' LOUNGE

MY DREAM OF BECOMING a professional footballer had been dashed in my teens. But in 2014 I got the opportunity to experience the next best thing: I became a director of a club.

I played for a Sunday morning team with a guy called Danny Wright whose brother, Tommy, had played for Leicester City as well as a string of other clubs before joining Corby Town, in the Southern League Premier Division, as a player-manager. Tommy invited me to a meeting with several other local business leaders at Steel Park, the club's ground, to discuss sponsorship. Corby Town was in crisis as Kevin Ingram, the owner, had put it into administration, claiming the local council owed the club £200,000 for managing the Rockingham Triangle Sports Complex, next to the stadium.

Seven of us attended the meeting and we each agreed to put money in to rescue the club. My initial contribution was £7,000. Paul Glass, who ran a recruitment agency, was also at the meeting; he was to become a good friend. We all agreed to give Tommy Wright sole charge of the first team.

Aside from the buzz of being involved in the running of a football club, I was always looking for new ways to bring more business to my own company, and I thought being a director might produce opportunities. I managed to put our stamp on the club when the boardroom was named the Utility Bidder suite.

I didn't know anything about how non-league football clubs worked, but I quickly learned that football at this level was a million miles away from the glamour and big money of Premier League clubs. With teams like Corby, money is tight and every penny counts. To save the club money, I secured a better deal for its electricity. The club shared an electricity meter with Rockingham Triangle, which led to disputes about how much energy each used and how much each should pay.

Volunteers are the lifeblood of clubs: they operate the turnstiles, sell programmes, work in the shop and do all sorts of other stuff behind the scenes. They do this because the club means the world to them. Corby has loyal supporters who go to every home game and even to many of the away games; the club almost always puts on a coach for away games, no matter how far away they are.

Unlike in the Premier League, non-league grounds are mainly terracing, so most fans stand. You can have a beer and you can move around the ground. Many home fans switch ends at half-time to get behind the goal Corby are attacking.

Most of the players at Corby were non-contract and paid weekly. If they weren't performing well, the club would get rid of them. If a player was on contract, it meant the club had to pay him if he got injured, which wasn't the case if he wasn't on contract. The players all had other jobs, usually involving flexible work. In some cases, employers would agree to give them time off for games. In fact, a couple of guys who once worked for Utility Bidder had played for Corby, and I had no problem giving them time off when they had a midweek away game. Most of the players didn't live in Corby, so they would drive to away games, usually car-sharing.

Not many players make it from non-league football to the top level, although no doubt many dreamed of doing so. Sheffield Wednesday bought Jordan O'Brien, a promising striker, from Corby, but unfortunately he didn't make it and returned to us. One of the few players who has made it at the top level is Jamie Vardy. Leicester City signed him in 2012 from Fleetwood Town for £1 million, a record for a non-league player; he had spent nine seasons playing non-league football.

I used to go and see Tommy at the training ground each week and chat to him about how things were going and who in the squad was looking good. He was paid for being the manager and also for running the academy. Managers at this level need a second income; they can't survive solely on what a club pays them, which is why a lot of managers take on coaching jobs.

Corby was one of the first academies in the area, but now there are loads of them. Because they are government-funded – with the provider paid per participant – academies can be good income generators. At its height, the Corby Town Academy had sixty kids in it, but at the time of writing, it only has twelve, so we'll be lucky to break even.

Academies give young teenagers something to do. I would have loved to be in one when I was sixteen. And a few lads do break through. Many clubs will try to have a couple of academy players on the bench, but it's very hard to make it in the football league. You see some lads who are excellent players, but they don't get near any football league teams. With the competition so fierce, you need to be better than excellent to have a chance of breaking into the professional game.

Being a director has given me a real insight into how ruthless football can be. For example, if Tommy wanted to sign a striker who cost £300 a week, he'd have to find £300 from his budget, which might mean getting rid of a couple of players. The players would be called into his office and let go that same day.

In my first season at Corby, I went to every game. To look the part of a director, I wore a suit along with a Corby Town tie. Usually when I went to football matches, I dressed casually. As a director, I got to meet the directors of other clubs in the directors' lounge, where food and drinks are usually provided after a game.

Probably the longest distance for an away game was Truro in Cornwall: six hundred miles there and back. We were winning 2–1 with four minutes of normal time to go. Then the floodlights failed, and the referee abandoned the match. Everyone from Corby was gutted. The FA ordered that the game had to be replayed, which meant not only having to make that long journey for a second time but also the club having to pay for hotel accommodation for the players and officials. And we lost the replay. It was devastating.

With ten games to go, Corby were ten points behind the league leaders. But we put together a good run, losing only once in the next nine games. A 1–0 win away at Weymouth meant we were only one point behind leaders Poole Town, which was our last game of the season. We had to win to get promoted to the National League North, which included teams such as Stockport County and FC United of Manchester. Poole just needed a draw.

I travelled to the match on the players' coach. I felt so excited, but, to my surprise, the players appeared extremely relaxed. Over 2,200 fans had packed into Poole's small stadium, many of them Corby fans, and some were in fancy dress. The atmosphere was electric when the teams came out on to the pitch. Corby won 3–2. When the final whistle went, the Corby fans erupted. The atmosphere was incredible in the changing room after the match.

We had a party when we got back home. A few days later, the council arranged an open-top bus parade from Steel Park to the Corby Cube – the landmark building in the town that contains the council headquarters and other civic amenities -- and I joined the players on the bus. On some of the streets there was only a handful of people cheering us, so it felt a bit strange. However, when we reached the Cube itself, several hundred fans had gathered. Afterwards, the mayor held a civic reception.

To generate income for the club, Tommy came up with the idea of holding summer tournaments featuring players from the squads of major clubs. Previously, the club had had pre-season games against clubs such as Leeds United and Nottingham Forest. These games attracted good crowds and the club made a bit of money. Liverpool, PSV Eindhoven, Porto, Newcastle United and Leeds United all took part in the tournaments. All the players were under-23s. Tommy was con-vinced we'd attract their fans, who lived locally. However, we only got crowds of between five hundred and six hundred, when we needed at least a thousand to break even. As we had to pay the travel and accommodation costs of each club, we lost money.

Corby started well the following season in the National League North, unbeaten in their first six games. There was a real air of optimism among the fans. But then it all went wrong after we lost 3–1 at home to Solihull Moors. We slipped further and further down the table and ended up being relegated to the Northern Premier League.

Another season resulted in another relegation.

After a poor start the season after that, Tommy lost the confidence of the hard-working chairman Steve Noble and Paul Glass, and they were thinking of sacking him. They asked me if I would speak to him. This was difficult for me, as I had a good relationship with Tommy and considered him a friend. He had built a good academy at the club, providing valuable income for it. If he left, there would be no one to run the academy.

I spoke to him on the Friday, the day before the home game against Ilkeston Town.

'Tommy, I'm really sorry, mate, but the board is considering letting you go,' I said.

'Yeah, I know it's not been a great season,' he said.

'I mean, you did brilliantly three seasons ago.'

'Yeah, well, that's football for you, James. Listen, if we don't win tomorrow, I'll walk myself.'

We lost 2–1. At the end of the match, I went to speak to Tommy, feeling nervous as I approached him. He told me he'd changed his mind and he was going to stick it out. But Steve and Paul weren't happy with that. The next day, I had to phone Tommy and tell him he'd been sacked. It was horrible, but I think he'd expected it. It all went a bit sour after that. He joined Nuneaton Borough and tried to poach some of our academy players. In 2020, he rejoined Corby Town as manager but resigned after two months. Following that, he quit football and became a police officer.

Going from champions to back-to-back relegations

illustrates how rapidly the fortunes of football clubs – and managers – can change. Tommy had been a hero one season and a villain the next. In that respect, at least, non-league football is no different to the Premier League.

With managers on contract, you can end up paying them even when they've left the club. This happened in 2021 when Gary Mills was sacked after Corby only finished fifteenth in the Division One Midlands of the Northern Premier League, despite having one of the largest budgets. Because of the contract he'd signed, the club had to pay him a weekly amount for the following season to get rid of him. Paying a manager who is no longer at the club is obviously a big drain on a small budget.

The big question for small clubs such as Corby Town is how to generate enough money to keep going. As I quickly discovered, there's no easy answer to that. If you get into the proper rounds of the FA Cup, that can be lucrative, but that doesn't often happen for the Corby Towns of football.

While chatting to Paul Glass at the club one Saturday afternoon, I mentioned that I was struggling to recruit the right kind of staff in the Market Harborough area. He suggested I move Business Energy Consultants to Corby. The previous year, both Business Energy Consultants and Utility Bidder had moved to Woodcock House at Compass Point Business Park on Northampton Road, as we had forty staff and needed more space. Woodcock House was a new building with good facilities. It was also across the road from the leisure centre, which meant the staff could go there at lunchtime if they wanted. However, Paul said it would be easier to recruit staff in Corby, which had one of the highest youth unemployment rates in the country. Paul's recruitment agency was involved in a scheme called Wise Up For Work, which worked in partnership with

Corby Jobcentre to train young people and help them find employment with local companies.

I raised the possibility of a move to Corby with Gavin, and he thought it could be a good idea. Like me, he was concerned that it was becoming hard to recruit the right kind of staff. Quite a few people in Market Harborough had worked for us at one time or another, meaning the pool of potential new staff was small.

Paul introduced me to Chris Mallender, chief executive of Corby Borough Council. He had been responsible for building Corby Cube and also a new ground for Corby Town. He told me he knew of an office that was available to rent at Corby Innovation Hub, an attractively landscaped business park containing offices, workshops and warehouses in the east of the town. When I went with him to see it, I was blown away. The office was on one floor and was about 10,000 square feet. It had meeting rooms and was ready for immediate occupation. It was better than any other office space I'd seen previously. The rent that Chris quoted was reasonable, and he added that we might get a council grant if we moved Utility Bidder to Corby.

Gavin and I duly did a presentation at the offices of North Northamptonshire County Council and talked about how many jobs we were going to create in Corby. As a result, we were given £30,000 towards our moving costs. Although we had signed a three-year lease with the landlord of Woodcock House, I was able to negotiate a deal with him to let us terminate it early. Most of our staff were from Market Harborough, and we had to convince them to travel to Corby, which was eleven miles away. All but one of them decided to come with us.

Moving from Market Harborough to Corby was a bit like

West Ham moving from Upton Park, an old ground, to the modern Olympic stadium. The facilities at Corby Innovation Hub were brilliant. However, I felt we lost all the atmosphere we'd previously worked so hard to build in Market Harborough, simply because the new office was so big. We had 30 people in 1,500 square feet in Market Harborough, and the place was buzzing when you walked in. Now, the team was all spread out around the space, so the office felt much quieter.

In 2015 Gavin and I agreed that Business Energy Consultants and Utility Bidder should merge to form one company, because it didn't really make sense to have two companies doing the same thing. Between the two companies, we were handling 7,000 energy bills a year. Gavin and I were ambitious to create a much larger energy company, which would mean hiring more staff. Some brokers employed between 150 and 200 people, and we thought maybe we could make Utility Bidder just as big.

I sought some advice from a tax specialist, who advised me to put Business Energy Consultants into voluntary liquidation, which we proceeded to do, using a liquidator in Leicester. When you liquidate a company, its assets are used to pay off its debts. Any money left goes to the shareholders. Sally and I received around £200,000 each, which was taxed at entrepreneurs' relief. I went out and bought a brand-new blue Audi A5. This was the first and only time I've bought a new car. The staff in both companies were all given new contracts and terms and conditions.

Recruiting the right staff and retaining them is one of the biggest challenges when you run a company. If you recruit the right people, they can help you make money. Recruit the wrong ones, and they will lose you money. Both Business Energy Consultants and Utility Bidder had always struggled to find the right staff. We had some people who had been with us for several years, but there had been many others who had only stuck around for a few months and then left. We had no problem recruiting staff, but many left, either because they didn't like the work or because we hadn't trained them properly. I found that, for every ten staff you employ, usually only two will turn out to be any good. This is probably true for anyone in the energy industry.

Taking on staff with no experience in the energy industry means you have to provide then with the right kind of training, which takes time and resources. We had not always done this properly, although we always tried to treat our staff well. For example, we would pay our sales agents up front each month for the contracts they sold, even if we weren't paid up front by the supplier. It was a way of helping sales agents earn more and build trust in us, which meant they were less likely to want to leave us.

When we were tipped off that some of the top sales people in British Gas were having their commissions cut, we took on eight of them, thinking they'd be brilliant as they knew the industry so well. However, even though they knew the energy market, they didn't all fit into our company culture. Some were lazy and used to a corporate environment. One morning, a guy phoned to say he wouldn't be coming in because he was taking a 'dependant's day'. I'd never heard this expression. I honestly thought he said Independence Day, and someone had to explain to me that it means having a day off when the kids are ill. That would of course be fine: take whatever time you need, mate. But do please call it what it is.

We now employed nearly sixty staff, and human resources was becoming a headache, so we brought in a company called Peninsula to take it over. It was a good move. They checked all our documentation and employment contracts and gave us support if we had a problem with any of the staff.

We also started using a database for the first time. We'd been using Microsoft Excel and Outlook to manage the details of our customers since 2007, but we recognised that we needed a better system. It took us a while to find the right one. I also began to realise that marketing – something I had barely paid any attention to – was important if the company was going to grow, so I hired a woman called Maddy and put her in charge of it.

In addition, I brought in a business consultant called Stuart, who had been recommended to me. Consultants are usually brought in by businesses that are struggling. After he discovered how well Utility Bidder was doing, he said, 'So, why do you need me?' I replied, 'I just want us to be better.' This was what I'd always strived for; I wanted Utility Bidder to be the best and most successful energy company. Stuart wasn't actually with us for long, as he was shocked by some of the language he heard from the sales team. I told him it was stuff we'd come to regard as banter.

We also brought in Robin, from Funding Options, a government scheme to promote growth for entrepreneurs, to help us with our finances, which were in a total mess. Gavin and I had trusted suppliers to pay us, but then we discovered some hadn't done so. We needed a system to reconcile contracts with payments.

Every day was non-stop, from the moment I arrived at the office until the moment I left. A good deal of my time was spent in meetings of one sort or another. I got through endless cups of coffee to keep me going. To get away from it all for a while, I would always try to get to the gym at lunchtime.

I never really dwelled on the fact that I was responsible for the company bringing in between £400,000 and £500,000 a month just to break even. I simply worked flat out each day. I didn't want to think about the fact that the livelihoods of all my staff depended on me. That would have done my head in.

We provided a few thousand pounds in sponsorship to Corby Town, which meant that Utility Bidder's name was on the shirts. If we got a few deals as a result of this, then we would make up the money we'd spent. If we didn't, then at least we were helping the club stay afloat and doing something for the local community. Over the years, I've got involved in sponsorship deals with various other organisations, ranging from the National Federation of Fish Fryers and bowls clubs to Cricket Scotland and Scottish Squash. The idea, of course, was that, in return, the organisations would promote Utility Bidder among their members.

At around this time I also set up an insurance company with Gavin, Sally and an insurance expert of Gavin's acquaintance. However, when the underwriter carried out a criminal record check, my conviction for using counterfeit money came up, and I was informed I couldn't be a director, so I had to resign. I was surprised that my record would be a problem, because the conviction was spent. But, to be honest, I wasn't that bothered, because I already had more than enough to keep me busy. As it turned out, the insurance company wasn't a success.

It's normal to have failures in business. What's important is that you learn from them and don't give up.

13

ENTERING INTO THE SPIRIT

As I've previously stressed, if you want to create a success-ful company, you need to find the right people. Once you've found them, if you want to retain them, you need to motivate them, provide incentives and make them feel valued. And, of course, you need to pay them well. If your staff are happy to go to work each morning, they will perform well. And if they perform well, the company will do well. Whatever business you're in, the people who work for it are its most valuable asset. It doesn't matter what systems or technology you have; at the end of the day, you need to remember that you are employing human beings, not robots.

You often hear people complain that they just feel like a number in the company they work for. Since Business Energy Consultants and Utility Bidder started, Gavin and I had focused a lot on making both companies fun places to work, and we'd invested in team-building activities. This went right back to the early days, when Gavin would take staff to the pub on a Friday after work.

My approach was simple. I wanted the staff to show respect and work hard. If they did, I treated them well. Our aim was to make those who worked for Utility Bidder never want to leave. We also wanted them to tell their friends that we were a fantastic company to work for. To that end, we put photos of various company activities on one of the walls in the office: the idea was to show visitors the fun activities the staff got involved in, as well as to help create a positive atmosphere in the office.

One summer, we hired the King Power Stadium, Leicester City's home ground, for a match between Utility Bidder and Buzz's work team, which cost about £3,000. I appointed myself player-manager. I'm happy to say that Utility Bidder won 2–1. We had a presentation at the end of the match and champagne was sprayed everywhere. Playing in the stadium was an incredible experience, even though there were only about seventy spectators. The slight downside was that the pitch hadn't been watered, so it was like playing on concrete, but we tried not to let that bother us.

I also organised games for the staff at MK Dons' stadium in Milton Keynes and on one of the pitches at the Leicester City training ground, where we had a six-a-side tournament with teams from other local companies. And I took staff on various hospitality packages, which I bought from my mate Friz's company, Imperial Corporate Events, such as to Royal Ascot, the Henley Regatta and Leicester races, where there would often be a concert or DJ. Everyone always had a brilliant day out.

I've also enjoyed corporate hospitality at major sporting events from suppliers such as CNG, British Gas and

Gazprom, including going to the Champions League Final at the Millennium Stadium in Cardiff. Suppliers have often provided us with hospitality packages for sporting events, and I've taken members of staff to them as well. One year, I took three or four of the team to the Oktoberfest, a German beer festival in London. Everyone sits at long tables and you're served large tankards of beer by waiters and waitresses in traditional German dress. When we left, we were all totally drunk.

I'd always looked for charity events in which staff could take part with minimal training. Utility Bidder teamed up with the Teenage Cancer Trust and we did a charity bike ride from Corby to Skegness a couple of times. The journey was seventy-five miles and took around six hours. It was reasonably flat most of the way, and we had support vehicles with us, so I found the ride pretty easy. A coach then took everyone back to Corby. The event raised nearly £4,000.

Taking on the Three Peaks Challenge was a different matter. The three peaks in question are the highest mountains in Britain: Ben Nevis in Scotland, Scafell Pike in England and Snowdon in Wales. The challenge is to climb each of them, one after the other, in twenty-four hours. Factoring in the journey times between them, this meant completing Ben Nevis in five and a half hours, Scafell Pike in four and a half and Snowdon in four. In all, we would hike 24 miles and drive 1,000 miles.

The idea for us to attempt this feat had come from Paul Marlow, the head of fundraising at Lakelands Hospice. Paul was really into outdoor challenges and had run several marathons. He was putting together a team to raise money and he suggested that Utility Bidder do the same. He told me that anyone could do the challenge if they had a reasonable level of fitness. I considered myself to be pretty fit, so I thought I'd have no problem completing it. I had no idea just how tough it would be.

Ten staff eagerly signed up. My dad also said he'd like to take part. Given that he was now in his mid-sixties, I wondered about the wisdom of this. Yet I reminded myself that not only had he done the Skegness charity bike ride, but he'd also cycled from London to Paris and from Paris to Marseille.

We all left Corby early one morning in August in two minibuses for the eight-hour journey to Ben Nevis, which is near Fort William. We all had warm clothing, hats, hiking boots, head and hand torches, flasks, bottles of water and snacks. There was plenty of joking and laughter as we travelled up the M6 to Scotland. Our plan was to start the climb up the mountain at four o'clock.

Our guides were waiting for us when we arrived at the Ben Nevis Visitor Centre. They explained we'd would be doing the hike in two groups. I have to admit that as I stared up at the mountain, it looked pretty daunting. I'd never gone up anywhere so high before. The guides warned that coming down could actually be more difficult than going up, as we would have to take long strides to prevent ourselves from slipping.

After leaving the car park, we crossed a bridge over the River Ness, walked down a narrow lane, passed through a stile and then found the path leading up the mountain. I was in the first group. Although the path was uneven, I didn't find the climb that difficult. As the path got steeper, my dad and a couple of others in the second group began to lag behind, struggling to keep up. At one point, we lost sight of that group. When we reached the top of the mountain, just before sunset, I felt a real sense of achievement. Eventually, my dad and everyone in the second group arrived.

'You made it, Dad! Well done,' I said.

'But my legs are paining me,' he said with a grimace.

'Just sit down for a bit.'

'James, I don't think I'm going to be able to make it back down.'

'You'll be okay.'

'No, seriously. I'm in real pain.'

If my dad really couldn't make it down, then we'd have to call an air ambulance. After I explained the situation to the guides, they said they'd support him on the descent.

My dad put an arm around a shoulder of each of the guides and unsteadily began the journey back to the bottom of the mountain. Going back down the mountain did indeed mean I had to take huge strides, and it wasn't long before my hips were hurting. It was pure agony. I realised I hadn't done enough training. We had all been expected to train every week before the event, but I could now see that we hadn't taken this anywhere near seriously enough. One week, training had consisted of nothing more than a walk around Corby.

By the time we all reached the bottom of Ben Nevis, my dad said he was okay now and was ready to tackle Scafell Pike. Paul told him it was too risky for him do it. When we arrived at the English mountain, my dad was still insisting that he was going to climb it, but Paul refused to let him go. The rest of us began the ascent, but we only got about three-quarters of the way to the top when Paul decided to abandon it, as we were behind time and he wanted to get to Snowdon.

I was absolutely shattered after I came down Scafell Pike, and I could tell some of the others were as well. I said to my team: 'If you don't want to do Snowdon, don't be embarrassed. I'm happy to drive you back to Corby.' Half of them, including my dad, said they wanted to do this. As I saw it, even if we had gone up Snowdon we would have failed the challenge, as we wouldn't have completed it in 24 hours – aside from the fact that we hadn't gone all the way to the top of Scafell Pike. So I got in the van and took half of the party back to Corby. When we got there, I celebrated our return by taking everyone to Nando's.

As another way to incentivise our sales team, we told them that once they'd hit their target for the week, they could go home. While this was a good idea in theory, it created resentment among the admin staff, who had to remain in the office to deal with all the contracts. Often there was friction between the two teams: sales weren't happy if admin returned a contract, and admin weren't happy with sales when they made a mistake with a contract. Trying to keep both teams happy wasn't easy.

I've always done my best to treat all the staff fairly and equally, but if you have a superstar sales person bringing in a million pound's worth of contracts a year, you don't want to lose them. So if they cause a problem, you'll perhaps be more understanding than you would with someone in a different department.

One Saturday afternoon at Corby Town, Paul Marlow said to me, 'You know, James, you should do the Strictly event in October.' He was talking about 'Strictly Corby', a version of the BBC's *Strictly Come Dancing*, which raised funds for the hospice.

I laughed. 'You must be joking.'

'Why?'

'There's absolutely no way you're going to get me dancing in front of people.'

I'd never been into dancing. Like a lot of blokes, I have two left feet and mastering steps was well out of my comfort zone. Signing up for the Ultra White Collar Boxing, I'd felt it was something I could do without making a fool of myself. This was a very different matter. I could think of no better way of making a prize idiot of myself than taking to the dance floor in front of an audience.

But whenever I saw Paul, he kept asking me to take part, and he told me he'd found a dancer who would coach me. Eventually, I threw caution to the wind and said I'd do it. I thought that it might be good publicity for Utility Bidder. It would also be a challenge.

My dance coach was Tori Nowlan, who was based at MaSh Dance Studio in Kettering. She would work with me for ten weeks and then dance with me on the night, when we would have to do a waltz, a cha-cha and a show dance. I would be one of ten local 'celebrities', five men and five women, taking part in an evening at the Best Western Rockingham Forest Hotel.

Tori was a good teacher, but I found the dance moves very hard, so I practised a lot at home. On the evening of the event, I arrived at the hotel, dressed in a black tailcoat suit, feeling very anxious. I was petrified of making myself look a complete pillock in front of the audience.

We all had to stand behind a curtain and wait for the *Strictly* music to begin. Tori, of course, was relaxed and couldn't wait to start. That made one of us. Stepping out from behind the curtain with her to dance the waltz, I was shaking. Tori moved around the floor effortlessly. There was no way I could match her. When dancing, you are thinking about your steps all the time and trying to match your partner. Boxing isn't like this.

After the waltz, I sat down and, to steady my nerves, I took a few sips of rum from a small bottle I'd slipped into my bag. The show dance was to a song from *Dirty Dancing*. After that came the cha-cha. When all the dances had finished, the judges scored everyone. It turned out I hadn't made a complete fool of myself after all. Having relaxed into the competition, I was actually quite disappointed to come second. But the event made nearly £60,000 pounds for the hospice, of which I raised £15,000.

Christmas parties have always been a big thing at Utility Bidder, and we've often given them a theme. One year, at the Best Western Hotel in Corby, we did our version of the TV show *Stars in Your Eyes*. Several staff volunteered to perform, and Paul Marlow agreed to compere it.

I decided to surprise everyone by appearing as Beyoncé, performing 'All The Single Ladies' as she'd done at Glastonbury. Everyone knew I planned to do something, but they didn't know what. My singing voice is awful so there was no way I was going to try to sing. Instead, I would mime. But the dance moves obviously had to be real. To prepare for my performance, I had lessons with Tori, who taught me the full routine. I took it all extremely seriously, spending hours practising at home. I was the last act on, so everyone, including me, had had a fair bit to drink. As I made my entrance, dressed in a black leotard and long blonde wig, all the staff began whooping and cheering. I started to get into the role and, by the end, I'd convinced myself that I was putting on a pretty decent Beyoncé performance. I got so into it that I stayed in costume for most of the rest of the evening. Sadly, despite all my efforts, I didn't win the competition. With hindsight, this oughtn't to have come as a surprise: I've now seen the video and I was actually pretty terrible. Still, it was a bit of fun and it gave everyone a good laugh.

At another Christmas party we had a German theme; I hired an oompah band, and some of the ring girls from the boxing shows served the beer. First, we held our annual awards ceremony. Jag from British Gas and Mike from CNG had come along to do the presentations. Everyone had been asked to dress smartly for the occasion and afterwards we would all get changed into traditional German costumes. However, in the middle of the ceremony, the door opened and Gavin appeared already wearing his German costume. We all broke into fits of laughter.

Getting staff involved in events outside of working hours is a fantastic way of helping them bond with each other, have lots of fun and develop a positive company culture. If you can do this, it will help you to build a successful business. I can't repeat this too often: it's all about finding and keeping the right people.

Speaking of which, someone was about to join Utility Bidder who would help me to achieve a financial success I'd never imagined.

14

A SURPRISE APPROACH

ONE MORNING IN SEPTEMBER 2017, I received a call from a guy called Chris Shaw, who offered to do some consultancy work for Utility Bidder to identify ways to grow the business. I had no hesitation in saying yes.

I'd met Chris through his colleague Andy Blake at Cheltenham Racecourse, where I'd been invited by British Gas. Andy had mentioned that Business Advisory Service, of which Chris was the CEO, was interested in buying a telesales company. I'd considered selling Utility Bidder, but only if the price was right. I'd asked Andy if he'd introduce me to Chris, so we could have a chat.

A couple of weeks later, we met at a hotel in Birmingham. I talked to Chris about Utility Bidder and how it had grown over the years. He asked a lot of questions, and I was impressed by his grasp of the business and how it worked. He was the first person to introduce me to EBITDA, which stands for 'earnings before interest, taxes, depreciation and amortisation'; it's a tool used to measure a company's financial performance.

Chris asked how many staff we employed, what was our average uplift – i.e. how much money we made on each kilowatt of energy sold – and what was our average length of contract. Gavin and I had never really thought about all of this, so we gave him some loose numbers. Chris said we needed to track our contract lengths and uplifts on a weekly and monthly basis. Gavin and I didn't really understand our numbers in this way. We both had plenty of business expertise, but not in how finance worked, which is crazy if you think about it.

At the end of the meeting, both Gavin and I felt we didn't really know our stuff, and we should have done. Despite this, though, we were making £7 million in sales a year.

Chris had phoned me because he'd left Business Advisory Service and was looking for new opportunities. I agreed to pay him twenty grand for a month's work. He said he'd do a full review of the business and look at how we could grow it. At the end of the month, I offered him a full-time position as CEO with the company to help grow it and then sell it. I would become managing director. Having Chris as CEO would relieve me of some of the pressures of running the company.

Chris said he'd take the job if we paid him a £180,000 basic salary, a 50 per cent bonus, a pension, and, as he lived in Lytham St Annes in Lancashire, accommodation in Corby during the week. I agreed to the package, as I believed Chris could help take the company to the next level. And it turned out to be one of the best business decisions I ever made. Bringing Chris on board was the equivalent of Leicester City signing a world-class striker.

Chris, Gavin and I had a meeting to discuss our roles and

responsibilities. In January, Gavin decided that he wasn't keen on the new direction of the business and told me he'd like to sell his shares. We came up with a company valuation of £7 million and I agreed to pay him a large instalment every month until I'd paid him his third. I ended up with 74 per cent of his shares, Sally 24.5 per cent and Richard – who had been incentivised over the years with shares – 1.5 per cent. After this, we shook hands, Gavin thanked me for securing his family's future and he left the company for good. I was aware, however, that I would still have to pay Gavin the money even if the company didn't do well.

One of the first issues Chris tackled was the implementation of a proper finance system. Our existing system was a mess, as our record-keeping had been poor over the years. He first brought in a consultant to help sort things out and then appointed a financial controller, Lisa Jones.

Chris and I had several meetings to put together a strategy for the company for the next three years. The company had never had a strategy other than improving on sales each year, which we always did. But we had nothing written down. We needed to decide where we wanted to go as a company and list some targets. Once we had done this, Maddy, our marketing lead, produced a PowerPoint display and I presented our strategy to the staff at the Christmas party. I explained that we aimed to double in size within three years, consider international expansion and look at acquiring other companies. Our performance targets for sales were £9.5 million in 2018, £12 million in 2019 and £20 million in 2020. Our planned investments included hiring a full-time trainer and a new financial controller. The presentation ended with our people plan, ENERGY:

Employ brilliant people – we want to be the best;

Never give up – we always want to win;

Ensure work is a place of fun – a place to learn and a place to develop;

Run it like you own it – take accountability, make good decisions and lead by example;

Go the extra mile – for your customers and each other;

You is we – together we are stronger.

As I figured some of the staff might have had too much to drink at the Christmas party and not taken everything in, I delivered the presentation again in January.

In May 2018 I received a LinkedIn request from Paul Mangan, an investment manager at a private equity company called Sovereign Capital.

Dear James,

I hope you don't mind me emailing you out of the blue, but I am keen to speak with you regarding Utility Bidder.

We are a UK investor with £920m under management looking for investment opportunities in mid-sized UK companies. Specifically, I am searching for businesses providing b2b energy monitoring and procurement services.

Our investment activity ranges from outright acquisition through to the provision of development capital and can include a combination of both cash out and capital for organic or acquisitive growth. We very much tailor our investment to the specific needs of the shareholders and the business.

We are continually looking for high-quality businesses to support. We would welcome the opportunity to have an informal conversation with you to learn more about the business and your plans, and to see if there might be something we can do together either now or in the future.

Would you be available for a conversation at some point in the coming weeks or so?

Kind regards

Paul

I didn't know much about the world of investment banking, but Chris did. When I spoke to him, he said there was no harm in having a chat with Paul. If I'm honest, I didn't really think anything would come of it.

I found out later that Sovereign had been unsuccessful in bidding for another energy company. While doing some research into the energy sector, they came across Utility Bidder and were interested.

I travelled to London with Chris for a meeting with Paul Mangan and two other members of the Sovereign team at their offices in Victoria Street. They asked lots of questions about Utility Bidder's income stream and other issues. Chris and I explained that we employed 90 staff, with more than 10,000 customers and a turnover in excess of £7.5 million. We had an office in Spinneyfields, Manchester, which we had set up when one of our sales team told us he was moving to the city. And Utility Bidder had just attained its water licence, following the deregulation of water in 2017, so it could now provide all the utility services to its customers across the country. There wasn't much profit to be made in switching water suppliers: you might save customers a couple of hundred quid a year and we'd make just sixty or seventy quid commission. But we had gone into water because we hoped customers might also switch their gas and electricity.

Paul asked us what our plans for the future were, how we were going to grow the business and how Chris had become involved. He said Sovereign was interested in how it could support our growth. After we came out of the meeting, I said to Chris: 'That all seemed positive, didn't it?'

'Yeah, but with investment companies you never can tell what's really going on,' he replied.

'Still, something could come out of it.'

'It's possible. You never know.'

I took his words to heart, dampening down my own expectations. At one time or another we had been approached by investment companies about buying the business, but nothing had ever happened. It would probably be the same with Sovereign, I thought.

Afterwards, we went back to our hotel, near St Pancras Station, and met up with Sally, Richard and a few others from Utility Bidder, who had come down to attend The Energy Live Consultancy Awards (TELCA), which is seen as the Oscars of the energy industry. Utility Bidder had been shortlisted for an award the previous year. I was due to be in France for the Euros at the time of the ceremony and wondered if I should cancel my trip to attend. I wrote an acceptance speech and put it on my phone, but in the end I didn't go, and Utility Bidder didn't win anyway. This time, I thought we must be in with a good chance of picking up an award, as we'd been nominated in four categories.

The event, to be held at the Honourable Artillery Company on City Road, was a black-tie occasion with a slap-up dinner. At awards events there's usually a speaker, a comedian and a DJ later on in the evening and often an after-party in a nearby bar where a room has been hired. The way awards work is that you have to pay to enter and suppliers sponsor the event. To attend, you have to pay for a table. The costs can stack up, but these events are good for meeting people in the industry and keeping up to date with things – with the caveat that if you ask people 'How's business?', you never know if their answer is true or not. As in any industry, competitors are cagey when talking to each other. But you also get to meet your suppliers or some new ones, and sometimes you'll be introduced to more senior people in a company, so on balance it's worth showing up. If you actually win an award, it boosts your standing in the industry, and you can mention it on your stationery and website. Awards can help bring you new business and they also make the staff feel proud to work for the company, which is good for morale. That's why I was delighted when I heard the compere announce that we had won the Sales Leaders of the Year award.

The day after the ceremony, I was due to fly with Tom to Russia for the World Cup semi-final between England and Croatia. Under Gareth Southgate, England were now looking like a team to be reckoned with. After coming second in their group, they had knocked out Colombia and Sweden. Croatia wouldn't be a walk-over, but I felt England could beat them.

I'd found a guy in Moscow who was selling tickets on eBay, and I'd arranged to meet him at a café in Moscow's Sheremetyevo Airport. He'd texted me his photo, so I would recognise him.

There were rumours about violent Russian fans, known as Ultras, planning to attack England fans, which had happened before and after England's opening Euro 2016 game in Marseille. Because of this, Sally didn't want me to go. I also had a dilemma: Hannah was due to graduate from Leeds University, where she had been studying primary education, on Monday and the World Cup Final was on Sunday. I phoned her and asked her if England got to the final, did she want to go. She immediately said yes.

I'd discovered that instead of flying direct to Moscow with British Airways, it would be cheaper to fly to Barcelona with EasyJet and take an Aeroflot flight from there. However, the EasyJet flight was delayed and we didn't land in Barcelona on time. I phoned Aeroflot and was told to go to its desk at the terminal. A surly young woman told me that, as we were too late for the flight, we'd have to book tickets on another one. She added that we'd also lost our return flights from Moscow to Barcelona. When I asked if we could have a refund, she shook her head and said Aeroflot needed twenty-four-hours' notice to change a flight. I had to buy tickets for another £600 each to a different airport in Moscow. I texted the guy I was buying the tickets from to tell him I'd be four hours late and flying in to Domodedovo Airport rather than Sheremetyevo. He told me to meet him in a café at Domodedovo.

When we eventually got to the airport, I spotted him straight away. He was a burly guy with a beard, wearing a black leather jacket.

'You got money?' he said.

'Yeah. Have you got the tickets?'

He nodded and patted his jacket pocket.

I was expecting him to hand me the tickets, but instead he said, 'Come this way,' pointing to the toilets.

I looked at Tom and whispered, 'Do you reckon it's a set-up?'

'Don't worry, if you're not out in two minutes, I'll come in.'

Feeling apprehensive, I followed the guy into the toilets. As I watched him reach reached inside his jacket pocket, I thought he might be going for a gun. But he pulled out the two tickets and handed them to me. I gave him the money. He offered to take us to our hotel, but I said we'd get a taxi. I had visions of us being driven somewhere and robbed – or worse.

We arrived at the hotel at around 11pm. The place was

like nothing I'd seen before: very glitzy, with an eighties feel. On the fourth floor was a nightclub with lap dancers. After checking in, we took a taxi to Red Square to see the Kremlin. I noticed that everyone appeared to be driving Škodas. It was exciting to see buildings I'd only ever seen on TV and which were associated with the Cold War. After wandering around for a while, we went to a couple of bars near Red Square and then returned by taxi to the hotel.

In the morning, we took the metro to the Luzhniki Stadium, the largest stadium in Russia, to the south-west of the city centre. Tom and I wore England shirts. We had to ask for directions several times, and people were very friendly and helpful. As for the game, Croatia beat England 2–1. It wasn't a great match. As ever, the trips to the matches can often be far better than the games themselves.

I cheered up, however, when I received an email from Paul Mangan at Sovereign, asking if he and some of his team could visit our office in Corby. I wondered where this all might lead. Would they be interested in buying Utility Bidder? I had no idea.

15

WHAT HAVE I DONE?

AT THE BEGINNING OF AUGUST, Paul Mangan, Rob King and Nate Janks from Sovereign paid a visit to our office to get a feel for the company. They talked to Richard and some of the sales agents and listened to some of the phone calls they were making. They seemed impressed by what they saw and heard.

Soon after, Chris and I travelled by train to London for a meeting with Sovereign.

'What do you reckon they'll do?' I said.

'They'll make an offer.'

'Are you sure?'

'Yeah.'

Chris was confident because he'd had a number of conversations with the team at Sovereign, and he felt discussions had gone well.

Sovereign were supposed to be the buy-and-build specialists. Their business model was to buy multiple companies and then sell them as a group. A buy-and-build strategy is commonly used by private equity firms seeking to expand operations, generate value and increase returns. It generally involves buying clusters of similar companies and combining them, thereby increasing their value.

When we arrived at Sovereign's office in Victoria, we were taken to the boardroom, where Rob King and several of his team were sitting at the table. Chris and I were both given a ten-page document.

'Listen, we really like the business and we want to make you an offer,' said Rob.

'Okay,' I said, wondering what kind of figure they would come up with.

'Yeah, great,' said Chris.

'I just want to run through a few things with you,' said Rob.

He talked us through the document, page by page. As we proceeded through the document, it was as nail-biting as a page-turning thriller: I knew the offer would be on the final page, but what would it be? Life-changing? Or insulting?

Finally we reached page ten and there it was, in black and white: Sovereign was offering £9 million up front and £3 million based on earn-outs. (An earn-out is a commonly used pricing mechanism by which the sale price of a business is directly linked to its future growth and success; the buyer and seller agree certain targets which, if achieved, will result in further payments being made to the seller.) This was fantastic – as good as I'd dared hope for.

I did my best to remain poker-faced. At the end of the meeting, Chris and I thanked Rob for the offer and said we'd consider the proposal. Then we went to a nearby café to discuss it.

'What do you reckon?' I asked.

'We can get more,' he said.

Encouraged by the strength of the offer, I could now see his point. 'I think so too,' I said. 'Do you think we can get them to £15 million?'

'We can definitely squeeze them for a few more million. I'll get back to them and say that they need to do a bit better.'

Negotiating the sale of a business can be risky. If you refuse an offer, the other party might decide to pull out. On the other hand, you naturally don't want to sell too cheaply. In the café, I did a deal with Chris. If the sale went through, he'd get 10 per cent of anything over £7 million on top of his £180,000 a year.

When we went back to our hosts' office, Chris told Sovereign we wouldn't sell for £9 million plus £3 million in earn-outs; they would have to improve their bid. It was a gamble, and we were both nervous as he gave our response, but it paid off. Sovereign upped its offer to £10 million up front plus £5 million from two earn-outs. To me this sounded brilliant. but afterwards Chris remained cautious and told me not to get too excited. He said that these deals often didn't go through because something turned up in the due-diligence checks; the other side would then withdraw its original offer, replacing it with a lower one, or pull out completely.

In September, Sally and I flew to Tenerife to celebrate my forty-second birthday. While we were there, Sovereign emailed me the heads of terms, the document setting out the terms of the deal agreed in the course of negotiations. While signing heads of terms doesn't bind you legally to selling a business, it does make it expensive to pull out (if, for example, you've changed your mind about selling or you've received a better offer). The other party can sue to get back the money they've already spent on carrying out due diligence.

By this time Sally had had enough of the business and

wanted to retire, so she she urged me to sign. But at the back of my mind I wasn't sure that I really wanted to sell. I held off for a few days. Eventually, though, I signed the document, had it scanned in the hotel and emailed it to Sovereign.

Even with heads of terms signed, there was no guarantee the deal would go through. The process of selling a business is similar to buying or selling a house when, for example, a bank might approve a mortgage in principle but then withdraw the offer if problems arise from the survey. Sovereign hired a large firm of corporate lawyers, Eversheds, along with the auditors Deloitte and a tax company, all of which which cost around £200,000. A virtual data room – a secure place for storing documents – was set up, and we uploaded all the requested information.

Chris stayed in Corby three nights a week during this process. Initially, I rented an executive apartment for him behind the Best Western Rockingham Forest Hotel. However, he found it too noisy, as the walls were paper-thin and people were coming and going at all hours, so I booked him a room in the hotel. He and I were seriously concerned that the deal wouldn't go through because of a number of energy claims we'd received. These had been brought by Business Energy Claims, which had been set up by a former energy broker who thought he'd found a legal loophole for customers to claw back the commission energy companies earned from the contracts customers had taken out. It was similar to the PPI claims. Business Energy claimed that because Utility Bidder was working on the customer's behalf, it had a duty of care to disclose commissions. But energy brokers never disclosed commissions; they sold energy. If a customer asked about commissions, they would be told they were included in the price, which was true.

We had to pay out on some of the claims, but the amount

wasn't huge. Naturally, we had to disclose the claims to Sovereign, who became concerned and sought legal advice, spending £20,000 on a barrister's opinion.

I was also concerned that my criminal record might affect the sale. When I asked my solicitor if I needed to mention it, he said I shouldn't, as it would now be considered spent. I wasn't so sure.

In November, Sovereign nearly pulled the deal because of the Business Energy claims. It was worried about the risks these might pose and wanted to know, in theory, how much we might have to pay back. It wanted to attach a number of conditions to the deal. If the sale went ahead, I wouldn't be able to take my money outside the UK, and escrow – the funds you deposit in a solicitor's account to be used in the event of any claims against you – would increase from £500,000 to £750,000 and go up from two to five years. Sovereign saw Chris as the main person to take the business forward. In addition, there would be a two-year earn-out. I would be paid 70 per cent of the agreed sale price and then have to hit targets to receive the other 30 per cent. Sovereign also said it wouldn't buy the business unless I reinvested. Chris and I agreed to all these conditions; we had no choice if we wanted the sale to go through. Sally and I agreed to buy 11 per cent of the company. We would put in £1 million on the day after the sale and £500,000 after each of the two earn-outs had been completed.

Finally happy with this, Sovereign invited us to the offices of Eversheds in Manchester on 20 December to sign all the legal documents.

The night before, we held the Utility Bidder Christmas party at the Holiday Inn in Corby. I usually loved our Christmas parties, where the staff could let their hair down and everyone could reflect on the successes of the past year. I enjoyed our annual awards ceremony and the more relaxed themed celebrations that always followed. This year, we had chosen the TV series *Peaky Blinders* as our theme. I had planned to do Peaky's speech from the scene where he says 'no fucking fighting'. I felt it was better not to say anything about the sale, which, Chris had said, still might not go through. Looking at the faces around me, though, I felt guilty.

The next day, Chris, Sally, Richard and I drove to Manchester. When we arrived at Eversheds' modern offices in the middle of the afternoon, we took the lift up to the sixth floor. Rob King and several other people from Sovereign were there, along with Sovereign's legal team and Andrew, our solicitor. Rob said his lawyers weren't ready, as they still had paperwork to go through and it was going to be a few hours before they were done, so we should go and get something to eat and come back at nine.

As it was the week before Christmas, the pubs and restaurants in Manchester city centre were packed and there was a party atmosphere in the streets. Eventually, we found a quiet Italian restaurant off Deansgate.

'Do you reckon it's going to go through?' I said after we'd ordered.

'Yeah, they won't pull out now,' said Chris, confidently.

'I don't know. I'm not so sure.'

'They've done all the due diligence. So that's it.'

'I hope you're right.'

'Don't worry, James, it will be fine,' said Sally, patting my hand.

We returned to Eversheds, but the lawyers still weren't ready, so we went to a nearby pub. Chris and Sally were in high spirits, but I felt strangely subdued. We went back to the office at just after eleven. This time, everything was ready. Laid out on a table in the middle of the room were dozens of documents, which I had to check and sign. I didn't look at all the paper. Legal documents are difficult to read; they're written that way deliberately. I just scrawled my signature, hoping that my solicitor had done all the necessary legal work. By the time I'd finished, it was nearly 1am.

'That's it,' I said as I signed the last document with a flourish, dropping the pen on the table. 'All done.' My hand was aching from having signed so many pieces of paper.

Everyone clapped and cheered. Sally gave me a peck on the cheek and, grinning widely, Chris slapped my back.

A guy wheeled in a silver trolley with bottles of champagne and glasses on it and people started taking photos and shaking my hand. It should have been the happiest moment of my life: I'd built a company from scratch and sold it for £15 million. Instead I had to force a smile, pretending to be happy. Far from wanting to celebrate my success, I was empty inside. I had been Utility Bidder; now I wasn't. It felt like a part of me had gone. Maybe it was just that I was exhausted after an emotionally strained and stressful few days, but the moment felt weirdly sombre.

It was nearly 2am when we left the office. I think we were all exhausted after what had been a roller-coaster day. Chris drove home to Lytham St Annes, and Sally, Richard and I took a taxi back to Market Harborough. I said little during the journey. I was still thinking about Utility Bidder no longer being my company. I'd been the managing director, in charge of a hundred staff and working twenty-four-seven. I had lived and breathed the business. My whole life had revolved around trying to make the business successful. Even football or playing golf had been connected to the business. Now that was all in the past. When Chris came on board, the plan had been to sell

Utility Bidder – but it had all happened much quicker than I'd expected.

The following day, Sally and I went to watch Dillian Whyte and Derek Chisora in a heavyweight boxing match at the O2 Arena in London, courtesy of British Gas, which had hired a private box and laid on all the usual VIP treatment. I met several other energy brokers, and they all congratulated me on selling Utility Bidder. I did my best to be upbeat about it, but deep down I regretted what I'd done. I couldn't say this to anyone, as they would have thought I was crazy, having just made so much money. I was also tired after what had been an emotionally draining and stressful few days.

The money from Sovereign went into my bank account on Christmas Eve. When I saw the amount credited to my account, I didn't jump up and down or anything. I simply thought, *What do I do now?* Basically, I had won the lottery. But I had no intention of buying flashy cars or a big house with a swimming pool. Those kinds of things have never really interested me.

I went back to work in the first week of January, after enjoying a few days of sunshine in Dubai, and called a meeting to announce that the company had been sold. I tried to present the news in a positive way, as I didn't want the staff to worry about their jobs. Everyone knows that when a company changes hands, there are often changes. I explained that we had secured an investment to build the business, but, deep down, it felt like I'd abandoned the ship. I saw the people in the room more as family than people who worked for me.

16

BUSINESS UNDER LOCKDOWN

EVEN THOUGH I'D SOLD Utility Bidder, I still went in to work
most days, as I wanted to make sure that the business achieved
the two earn-outs. Without the additional £5 million, the deal
with Sovereign wouldn't be so great.

Chris was running the business now, not me. Officially, I
was the managing director, but, in reality, I didn't have much
to do. I began to feel that my role was becoming smaller and
smaller, even though I was going into the office, attending
meetings with suppliers and board meetings with Sovereign.
Every couple of weeks, I would go to Manchester to see how
the team there were doing. It was good for them to see me, as
they could feel a bit cut off from operations in Corby. But I
hated the long drive up the M6. The journey was about three
hours each way, or longer if the traffic was bad. I'd leave at
half six in the morning and often not get back until seven in
the evening.

I was finding it difficult to adapt to not being in charge any longer. I was used to being the guy at the top, who kept everything running and sorted all the problems. For the previous nine years or so, my life had revolved around running Utility Bidder. It was more than a job; it had become a big part of who I was. I'd sought a purpose in life and discovered it running Utility Bidder.

I started to look for the best place for Sally and me to invest our capital from the sale of the company. I had meetings with my accountancy company, Tilney, as well as with Barclays Wealth Management and Coutts. I decided to go with Tilney, which had an arrangement with Credit Suisse that would enable me to borrow money against my investment portfolio. To invest the money, we set up a company, Langton Investments Ltd.

Frustratingly, however, Credit Suisse contacted me to say they had found out about my criminal record. This hadn't come up as an issue with Sovereign, but the Swiss investment bank told me that if I wanted to invest with them, I would have to resign as a director of Langton Investments. To protect my money in the company, I would then have to obtain a deed of trust, a legally binding document that set out the division of the money that Sally and I had invested. Credit Suisse told me that eventually I would be allowed to be listed as a director of Langton Investments. In the event, they didn't permit this, even though we followed all their instructions. We eventually closed the account.

We completed the first earn-out in the September, far quicker than I'd imagined. Despite the knockback over my past, things were looking good.

One day, I received a message on LinkedIn from a woman claiming to work for the Bulgarian government on the deregulation of the energy industry, to comply with EU regulations, and asking for advice. Initially, I thought it was probably a scam, but when I spoke to her on the phone, I decided she was genuine. She asked me if I would travel to the Bulgarian capital, Sofia, for a meeting with the country's minister of energy. It sounded like an interesting trip, and England were due to play Bulgaria in the Euro 2020 qualifier in Sofia while we were there, so I said I would, inviting Chris and Sally to come with me.

We flew to Sofia and booked into a city-centre hotel, which also housed a casino. Sofia was interesting, with its ornate churches with domes, historic buildings and monuments from the Communist era. This was the first time I'd encountered people riding electric scooters through the streets.

That evening, Sally and I went to the Vasil Levski National Stadium to see the England vs Bulgaria match. Unfortunately it was marred by racist chanting by some of the Bulgarian fans. The referee stopped the game in the twenty-eighth minute after Raheem Sterling was targeted with abuse. He stopped it again just before half-time, threatening to abandon the game. Despite all the abuse, England thrashed the home team 6–0.

The next morning, Chris arrived and we all hired scooters and, dressed in our business suits, headed off to the National Assembly building. The energy minister greeted us warmly and introduced us to his glamorous assistant. After we all sat down, Chris and I explained how switching worked, how energy suppliers encouraged it and how brokers and commissions worked. I thought: *What am I doing advising a Bulgarian minister?* It felt surreal.

The first time I saw reports on social media of Covid-19 ripping through Wuhan in China, and then hospitals in Italy struggling to cope with the number of people being admitted with Covid, I didn't think the UK would be badly hit. I spoke to Chris about it and he thought the same. There was no way the UK would have to lock down, we agreed.

Then Prime Minister Boris Johnson appeared on TV on 23 March and announced a twelve-week national lockdown to prevent the spread of the virus. Only essential shops would be allowed to open, and pubs and restaurants would have to close. Everyone was ordered to stay at home and only permitted to leave for essential reasons, such as buying food or for medical necessities. 'Stay home. Protect the NHS. Save Lives' was the slogan that accompanied the government's public health announcement. Suddenly, it felt like our freedom was being taken away by the government.

Given that many of our customers were in the hospitality sector, the lockdown was a massive concern for Utility Bidder. Contracts we'd signed with businesses were based on an estimate of the amount of energy use each year. If consumption fell below the estimate, the supplier would claw back a certain percentage of the money we'd been paid. This situation created a lot of uncertainty for the company. The value of the business was based on forecast revenue. But the last thing on most people's minds was switching energy supplier. The country was in a state of shock and panic at having to go into lockdown. With so many government restrictions, and queues at shops for food, it was no wonder people were likening it to life during the Second World War.

Utility Bidder still managed to sign up new customers. The pubs and restaurants might be closed, but the managers or owners often lived above their premises or had go in to their businesses for various reasons. If they didn't, we could still contact them if we had their mobile phone numbers.

Nevertheless, our business took a major hit. Utility Bidder had been doing £1.6 million sales a month. Because of lockdown, monthly sales now dropped to between £700,000 and £800,000. Our sales team tried to persuade customers to switch to five-year deals, as energy prices had dropped. But in a climate of such uncertainty, we didn't know how much of that money we would actually see. If pubs or restaurants who'd signed contracts with us were forced to close, then we'd lose money.

In order to keep going, Utility Bidder took out a Barclay's bounce-back loan of £800,000, and later on, Sally and I loaned the business £700,000 out of the escrow account. All the staff had to work from home. We used Teams and Zoom to keep in touch with each other and did weekly calls with Sovereign to keep them updated on the situation. Some staff were put on furlough. Unfortunately, with income falling and an uncertain future, others had to be made redundant.

I was worried that Utility Bidder might fail, but when I talked to Chris, he said, 'Listen, if you're worried about the earn-outs, everything's fine. We're going to hit the targets.'

Lockdown was tough for many people. I was fortunate to have a good set-up at the former farmhouse in Church Langton, a village just north of Market Harborough, which I had bought with Sally. I had a gym, a golf simulator which I'd had built in one of the old barns, and a pool table. With more time on my hands, I started training hard again. I also managed to buy a hot tub. I got a friend to pick it up, even though you weren't supposed to make non-essential journeys. There were stories of the police stopping cars and asking people where they were going. Another friend, an electrician, installed the tub.

We were all told to follow the 'hands, face, space' guidance when out in public. I was reluctant to follow all of the rules; I didn't believe in many of them. I felt the government was trying to scare people into doing what it wanted us to do. Because I wanted to travel, I was one of the first in the queue for the vaccine. However, I admired the tennis star Novak Djokovic for refusing to be vaccinated in order to play in the Australian Open. He said he was standing up for what he believed in.

My dad's partner, Kathleen, was so worried about catching Covid that she never went out. Any time I went to see my dad, she wouldn't even open the door. Covid changed her; she became anxious and stressed and was on a lot of medication.

As everyone was spending so much time at home, I started playing tennis with Buzz, Friz and some other friends in Welland Park in Market Harborough. I hadn't played much tennis before, although I'd had a few lessons on holiday in Tenerife with former pros. The tennis was great for bring-ing people together and keeping everyone's spirits up in what was a dark and uncertain time. To make things more fun, I organised a tournament, calling it 'Wellandon', and took bets on who might win. I created four leagues with play-offs: the Champions League, Europa League, Inter-toto and Zenith Data Systems. We didn't have umpires, which, inevitably, led to the odd argument over a line call, as we all wanted to win. At the end of the tournament, we had a party in our garden at Church Langton. I even invited a fantastic Rod Stewart tribute act to perform at it.

In May, after lockdown had ended, I drove to Manchester, which looked like a ghost town, and opened the office. I told the staff that if they wanted to come in, they could. I then opened the Corby office, giving all the staff the same message. I was desperate to get people back to work in order to hit the earn-out target.

In July, to encourage people to return to pubs and restaurants again, Chancellor Rishi Sunak introduced the Eat Out to Help Out Scheme. From Monday to Wednesday throughout the month of August, anyone eating at participating businesses would get 50 per cent off food or drinks, up to a maximum of £10 per head. For Utility Bidder, this was a good initiative. Despite all the turmoil and economic uncertainty, we ended 2020 with pretty good sales figures, which was remarkable. It was testament to how hard our sales team had worked and adapted to working from home.

I hadn't been sleeping very well for a while. Not sleeping at night means your whole day is ruined. I'd been to see my GP, who had prescribed sleeping tablets and it had got to the stage where I couldn't sleep without them. Early one morning, I got up and went downstairs and just lay on the floor. It felt like electric shocks were going through me. The previous day, I'd been in London for meetings, and I hadn't felt right then either. Lying down helped and the frightening turn passed, but I continued to feel run down and I found it hard to concentrate on anything. Sometimes, I felt I was struggling to breathe. At one point, I thought I was going to have a breakdown.

I went back to talk to my GP.

'What can I do for you?' he said.

'I just don't feel great,' I told him, and explained my symptoms in more detail.

'Do you sometimes feel depressed?' he asked.

'I certainly feel low sometimes,' I said.

'Why do you think this is?'

'I don't know.'

'What's been going on in your life recently?'

'I suppose the biggest thing is I sold my business.'

'Do you think this might be linked to your depression?'

'Possibly. I mean, it was a massive part of my life.'

'I see. Were you forced to sell it?'

'No. I sold it because I had a good offer.'

'So you've not had financial problems since selling it?'

'No, nothing like that. Quite the opposite, in fact. I made a few million.'

He raised his eyebrows. 'Oh, really.'

I could see he was struggling to understand how selling the business for so much money might be linked to depression. I didn't blame him. He must have thought I was living the dream.

He arranged for me to have blood tests, but the results didn't indicate any problems. He also suggested that therapy might help. I had some cognitive behavioural therapy sessions online, but then gave up, as they didn't help. For me, therapy was a waste of time. It gave me an opportunity to talk about my problems, but it didn't solve them. We often know the answers to our problems; the hard part is doing something about it. Making changes in your life isn't easy, no matter what the self-help books say.

Meanwhile, it seemed like Covid would never end. As the daily reports of the number of infections, hospital admissions and deaths went up and down, Professor Chris Whitty, the government's chief medical adviser, provided live televised briefings with charts and numbers. The government intro-duced restrictions and then eased them and then increased them. They changed so often it was hard to remember what they were.

I constantly found myself at a loose end, feeling I had nothing to do. Some days, I'd sit on a bench in the park or linger in a coffee shop. Sally was busy with the farm and the horses, but I felt I needed to get away. In January 2021, I asked her if she'd mind if I went to Dubai. She said that was fine. I promised I'd be back by April.

Paul Glass had a villa in Dubai, so I stayed with him. Being away from the UK was liberating. I went to the beach each day and set up a gym in an outhouse in the grounds of Paul's place. In the evening, I played pool and we had parties with some of his friends. I enjoyed the sunshine and the party atmosphere so much that I didn't want to go home, so I ended up staying for nearly two months.

The emirate was on the red list, which meant that when I returned to the UK, I'd have to isolate in a hotel for ten days. I didn't fancy that, so I began looking at returning via another country, which would allow me to quarantine at home. Egypt was on the amber list, so I flew to Cairo and then took an internal flight to the Red Sea resort of Sharm el-Sheikh, arriving at my hotel in the early hours of the morning.

When I went to breakfast with my face mask on, I felt foolish, as I discovered no one else was wearing one. What's more, there was no social distancing. Most of the guests were Russians or Ukrainians. One of the waiters told me he was amazed that an English person had come to the hotel. After a relaxing stay, I flew back to the UK – but not before I'd taken the opportunity to buy a couple of hundred sleeping tablets from a pharmacy.

In May, Sovereign undertook an audit of Utility Bidder. I was worried that something might come up that would affect the second earn-out. In the interim, however, I had something else to worry about: a High Court battle with the high-street book-makers Paddy Power.

I had found myself in a dispute with Paddy Power over a bet

I'd placed two years before during a golf holiday in Marbella with Chris, Richard and a few other guys. While I was there, Paul Glass texted me and asked me to place some bets for him because some of his accounts had been closed by gaming companies. He had a jockey friend who I suspected was behind the tips, because they tended to be very good: on the Friday evening, for example, we won £80,000. On the golf course the next afternoon, Paul kept texting me with the names of horses and I phoned Paddy Power with them. We lost £20,000. Then Paul phoned and said, 'Put as much money as you can on Redemptive in the seven twenty at Wolverhampton.'

I rang Paddy Power to ask for £1,300 each way on Redemptive, which was at 16/1: £1,000 from Paul and £300 from me.

'Wolverhampton seven twenty, yep,' said the operator.

'Thirteen hundred pounds each way, please.'

'Thirteen hundred each way. On what, please?'

'Redemptive.'

The operator put me on hold while she sought clearance for the bet from her supervisor.

'All right, so that's going to be £26,000 coming from Jameslongley1, is that correct?' she said, when she returned to the phone.

This was ten times more than a £1,300 each-way bet ought to cost. Bookmakers don't just accept any bet; they have to assess the risk. She seemed to be telling me that they had done their assessment and were prepared to take a wager tenfold higher than I had originally proposed, if I was game for that.

'That's it, yeah,' I replied, coming to a fast decision.

'Set for clearance.'

'Thank you.'

'And your bet is on. Fine, Mr Longley.'

'Lovely.'

When I checked this on the Paddy Power app, it confirmed that I had paid the larger sum. Since most of the stake was coming from Paul, I phoned him to tell him the news.

'If we win, we're going to get nearly £300,000,' I said. 'What do you want me to do?'

'Just leave it. I think Redemptive will get a place at least.'

Chris, who was with me on the golf course, said, 'James, you should get out of it. Don't make the bet.'

However, our other companions disagreed. 'No, leave it on,' they said.

We went to a bar near the beach to watch the race on TV. One of our party told some of the other customers that I had £26,000 on the horse. When Redemptive won, everyone in the bar went mental. Paul was ecstatic when he phoned me. He had run around his pool table at his villa in Dubai when the horse crossed the finishing line.

When I checked the Paddy Power app, it showed £286,000 in my account. I took a screenshot and sent it to Sally. To celebrate, I took everyone to the Rooftop Bar and bought all the drinks. I probably spent two or three grand.

The following day, I flew to Tenerife to meet Sally. We'd decided to spend a few days there. However, when I looked at my Paddy Power account on the Monday morning, the £286,000 wasn't showing. Instead, it had dropped to?? £28,600. I was puzzled – to put it mildly.

I phoned my account manager at Paddy Power to ask what was going on.

'I'm sorry, there's been a mistake,' he said.

'What do you mean?'

'Your bet should only have been for £1,300 each way.'

'But my bet was accepted at £13,000 each way.'

I carried on arguing with him, but he insisted the bet should have only been for £1,300. It felt like they weren't playing fair. If Redemptive had lost, would Paddy Power have been so keen to reduce my stake?

I happened to know the champion jockey Kieren Fallon quite well, as we'd played golf together, so I phoned him for advice. He suggested I speak to a lawyer called Christopher Stewart-Moore, who had represented him in several court cases. I phoned Christopher and explained what had happened. He told me that he thought I definitely had a case against Paddy Power. But as Paddy Power didn't allow more than one person to be involved in a bet, I would have to take any legal action on my own.

After I returned to the UK, I had a number of conversations with Christopher's son Harry, who had lots of experience in horse-racing cases and gambling disputes. Along the way, Paddy Power offered £3,000 compensation, but I turned it down.

Eventually, a date was set for a hearing at the High Court, in July, the day before the England vs Germany game at Wembley in the Euros, for which I had a ticket.

A few weeks earlier, I had met with QC Mark James at Temple Garden Chambers in London to discuss the case.

'How do you think it might go?' I asked.

'I'd say it's seventy-thirty in your favour,' he said.

'So, I've a good chance of winning?'

'In my opinion, but you can never say for sure what a judge will decide.'

'But, I mean, what's your hunch?'

'Well, I think it's quite likely that Paddy Power will settle before the case goes to court.'

'You reckon?'

He nodded. 'They won't want all the negative publicity. It's bad for their reputation.'

'That would be great.'

'But, of course, I can't say for certain that they will settle.'

I came away feeling upbeat. Mark seemed confident that I had a good case.

On the morning of the hearing, I met Mark at the High Court to run through our arguments. He said the case, which was being heard by Mrs Justice Ellenbogen, was likely to last two days.

Mark argued that I was entitled to £257,400, the difference between the £286,000 Paddy Power initially paid and its revised payment of £28,600. In court, he played a recording of the phone call between me and the operator, which began with me attempting to place a £1,300 each-way bet. He said that I had been fully aware that the operator had taken £26,000 from me, as I'd checked my account via the Paddy Power app before the race started.

'At that point he knew he had staked £13,000 each way on Redemptive at 16–1,' Mark stated, arguing that Paddy Power had contractually accepted my bet.

The barrister representing Paddy Power claimed that there was no valid contract, that Paddy Power had never intended to offer or accept a bet other than the one initially placed by me and that, as an experienced gambler, I should have known this. He told the judge that, although the bigger stake had been approved, there had been a mistake in the relaying of my actual intention, which was to place a bet with a stake totalling £2,600. He went on to say that Paddy Power had the right to adjust the bet under its terms and conditions, due to the phone operator's mistake in relaying the higher stake to the trader.

'Isn't it true, Mr Longley, that when you placed the bet on

Redemptive you only intended it to be £1,300 each way?' he said as he began to cross-examine me.

'No,' I replied.

'You didn't really know what you were doing, did you?'

'I knew exactly what I was doing.'

'The truth is that Paddy Power made an error and, having realised that, rectified it immediately.'

'It wasn't a mistake.'

'What leads you to that conclusion?'

'The agent asked me if I wanted to bet £26,000, and I said yes. She didn't ask me if I really wanted to bet that amount. She accepted it.'

'But, Mr Longley, your original bet was for £2,600.'

'I mean, this was obviously a significantly bigger bet than I had asked for, but I was very confident that Redemptive would do well in the race and so I was happy with the £26,000 bet.'

When I came out of court after the second and final day, I felt positive. I said to Mark, 'What do you think?'

'Fifty-fifty,' he said with a shrug.

It took nine months for the verdict to come out. When I read it, I was dismayed. I had lost the case. The judge had concluded that there was no legal contract. She said the mistake made by Paddy Power meant there was no valid offer and acceptance, which the law demands before it will recognise an enforceable contract.

Taking the case to the High Court was probably one of the worst decisions of my life. I ended up losing money because of the hefty legal fees. Once Paddy Power refused to pay up, I never felt quite right about going to court. But I had been advised to do it by my solicitor. I don't know if he and the barrister actually believed I had a good chance of winning, or whether they were just interested in the fees they would be paid. Taking a high-street bookmaker to court is a great story to tell in the pub, but I'd rather it had had a different ending.

During the 2022 World Cup in Qatar, I met a lawyer in a bar and told him about the case. After reading the notes I'd kept on my phone, he said, 'I have to say, the judge was right.' When I asked him why, he said that just because you agree something with someone, it doesn't mean there's a binding contract. There was no case law for the dispute I'd had with Paddy Power. The judge had looked at cases from a hundred years ago about errors in contracts over – believe it or not – the cost of buying and selling cow hides.

There was at least good news back at Utility Bidder, which finally hit the second earn-out. We now had to wait for Sovereign to approve it. I felt extremely anxious, as I was worried they might find some reason or other for not paying up. Chris, on the other hand, had no such concerns.

One morning, Rob King phoned.

'I've got some news, James,' he said.

'Yeah, go on,' I said, expecting the worst.

'The earn-out has been approved.'

'Seriously?'

'Congratulations. It can't have been easy doing this in the middle of the pandemic.'

This was the final piece of the jigsaw of the sale. It had taken two and a half years, and it had been an anxious time for me. But, finally, we had hit the target.

17

LESSONS LEARNED

I WAS NEVER CONVINCED that selling Utility Bidder was the right thing to do. And I just wasn't prepared for how I might feel afterwards. As I signed all those documents late at night in Manchester to transfer the company to Sovereign, it felt like I was selling a part of me.

Given the way that Utility Bidder keeps growing, I can see it being sold for between £40 million and £60 million in the not too distant future. A successful business is one that can overcome challenges and, where necessary, adapt. Utility Bidder achieved this through the Covid pandemic. And just as we were emerging from that crisis, the company faced another major challenge when Russia invaded Ukraine in February 2022.

The news that Putin might invade Ukraine didn't really register with me. I doubted he would do it. When he did, gas prices shot up. In a way, this was good for energy companies because energy was suddenly on the front page of all the newspapers, which got people thinking about the subject. If prices are low and nothing's happening in the energy market, most people give little thought to it. But an energy crisis forces them to do this. Having energy as the lead story on all the news programmes made people sit up.

The UK imports a lot of its energy, and Europe gets a lot of gas from Russia. After Russia invaded Ukraine, there was great pressure from governments in Europe to stop using Russian energy. We had worked a lot with Gazprom, which sold Russian gas. It was a good company to be involved with: its prices were competitive and they paid us on time. Following the invasion, a lot of customers said they didn't want to stay with Gazprom because it was Russian. We told them they could move if they wanted, but their prices would double or triple, and they'd have to pay a fee to be released from their contract.

Gazprom's staff in London weren't allowed to go to their office over fears that they might be attacked. Eventually, the company changed its name to SEFE Energy.

I never imagined energy prices would increase as much as they have. The rises are unprecedented. Many customers are worried they won't be able to pay and a lot of businesses have been crippled by the price hike. In 2022, some businesses that had been paying 15p per kilowatt were now paying £1.

During my career in the sector, we sold energy and tried to make a fair commission and give the customer the best advice we could. The rise in energy prices is partly to do with Covid, as companies stopped creating energy during the pandemic. When we came out of lockdown, things went crazy. Everyone was trying to get their hands on energy. At the time of writing, Utility Bidder is doing a record number of sales, but the value of the contracts isn't as good as it was before Russia invaded Ukraine. This is either because suppliers are not offering long-term contracts or because customers don't want them.

Whereas our average contract length used to be three years, it's now eighteen months. The energy market is a volatile one; suppliers need long-term certainty to give you long-term prices.

A lot of energy suppliers have gone out of business since the war in Ukraine started. Some of those on moneysupermarket.com were little more than a guy sitting in his bedroom supplying 10,000 homes.

If you were saving a customer money, a conversation about energy was an easy one to have. 'It's great news. We're saving you two grand a year.' Over the past couple of years, it's been more like, 'We've done a good job for you. Your bills are only going up two grand.'

What I enjoyed most about Utility Bidder was the people I worked with. I didn't find the energy industry particularly interesting. No one's going to thank you for changing their energy contracts. By contrast, some of the people who boxed in the shows I organised said the experience had changed their life.

Everything in my life had been built around making Utility Bidder successful. But success doesn't come easy. You have to work hard for it, overcome the obstacles in front of you and believe in what you're doing. Many of those who start a business give up at the first hurdle. If you read the autobiographies of people such as Richard Branson or Alan Sugar, you see how single-minded they were in wanting success.

Robert Kiyosaki says in his bestseller *Rich Dad Poor Dad: What the Rich Teach Their Kids About Money That the Poor and Middle Class Do Not!*, 'In today's rapidly changing world, the people who are not taking risks are the risk-takers.' If you've got a mortgage and kids, it's not easy to take risks. But after I came out of prison, I didn't see starting a business as a risk. I couldn't see another option, and I wanted to earn some decent money. Most of the risks I took at Utility Bidder were driven by gut instinct. If it sounded like a good idea, I did it. Nowadays at Utility Bidder, when it comes to taking a risk, this is done by analysing spreadsheets.

Looking back, I think it's incredible how Gavin and I managed to sell contracts in the early days, as we knew so little about the energy business. But we had identified a target market that knew even less than we did about energy. If I'm honest, our products probably weren't that good, but our timing was. We were selling something at the right time. This was sheer luck, and you need some of that in business.

Early in the life of a business, the only pressure you have to deal with is that which you put on yourself. But when you start to become successful, and you employ people, pressure comes from the outside. It's like the proverbial frog in boiling water: the pain increases gradually so you don't notice it. That was certainly true in my case.

When I started out in the energy business, it was a murky world where companies were not always totally honest with their customers. Nowadays, the industry is more tightly regulated and companies don't generally engage in the kind of underhand practices that once took place. Energy brokers now have to disclose commissions and tell customers what they'll earn from their contract over the next five years. Verbal contracts are no longer accepted. As well as these safeguards, a dispute resolution scheme has been launched.

If we'd had someone who could have given us guidance, Gavin and I could have done much better than we did. I don't know whether or not I had a vision for the company; it was probably more about just keeping going. Gavin and I both had something in us that propelled us onwards.

Our product required no outlay – unlike, say, a car dealership or a restaurant. A car dealer can have millions of pounds' worth of vehicles on their lot and never know when a customer is going to buy one. And every month, those cars lose value. Running a restaurant means you have to buy vegetables, meat, fish and so on, and you might not sell it all. We didn't have those problems.

Had we appeared on *Dragons' Den*, I'm pretty sure all the dragons would have said, 'I'm out.' We wouldn't have had a clue about our numbers, which are essential when you're being grilled by the TV experts. I can hear Peter Jones saying, 'Your valuation's crazy. There's no way I'm investing in this.' But *Dragons' Den* is all about obtaining an investment so you can grow your company. I never sought any investment or took out a single loan for Business Energy Consultants or Utility Bidder, even though we had cash-flow problems at times. Gavin and I overcame all the obstacles we faced, whether they were to do with finance, staff or anything else. We came through the 2008 financial crash unscathed because we had no debt and the price of oil and gas plummeted, which meant it was easy for us to persuade customers to sign up with a new supplier offering a cheaper deal. It was much harder for a lot of other businesses; some companies went to the wall and their owners and staff even lost their homes. But we grew, and as we did so, we became more professional. Departments such as IT and marketing became crucial in our achieving further growth.

As you can imagine, I'm often asked the secret of my success. How did I create a business from nothing and sell it for millions? What lessons in business have I learned along the way? I never did any kind of 'professional development' apart from reading books, watching YouTube videos and talking to people who were involved in businesses. What I learned, I learned through experience. Here are some of those lessons.

Robert T. Kiyosaki says in *Rich Dad Poor Dad* that you shouldn't say you can't afford something. Instead you should ask yourself how you can afford it. For example, if you can't afford to go on holiday this year, you need to think how can you make the money so that you *can* go. Or if you want to buy a house, then you need to work out how you can find the money to do this.

I remember as a kid saving up to buy a replica World Cup football. When I was playing on the green opposite my house, one of my friends accidentally kicked the ball on to the road and a bus ran over it. Initially, I was distraught because that ball meant so much to me. But then I thought, well, I just need to work hard to earn enough money to buy another one.

When I look back to those days when I did three paper rounds, worked with my dad and helped on a market stall, all at the age of thirteen, it's clear to me that I had an entrepreneurial approach to life. But I didn't realise that at the time. I was simply seizing opportunities to make some money.

Some people don't recognise opportunities when they come along. When I picked up Gavin in my taxi and he asked if I wanted to get involved in an energy switching business, I could have easily turned down his offer, especially as I was working all hours driving taxis. But I thought I'd give it a go.

To be successful means taking risks, but calculated ones. I've always started slowly, to see whether something worked or not. If you're someone in a nine-to-five job who dreams of running your own business, then test out your idea to see if it's viable. For instance, you could start by selling something online, or having a market stall at weekends, or, if you're planning to work with food, doing deliveries or pop-ups. Overcome the fear by starting small, recognising it as a stepping stone to significant achievements.

If you decide to quit your nine-to-five job, you need to make sure you have enough money to provide an income and cover your costs for at least six months. This might involve taking out a loan from the bank.

I never borrowed money at Utility Bidder and I never owed anyone a penny. Utility Bidder always had cash in the bank. On the upside, that meant I never had to pay interest to anyone, but maybe not borrowing was a mistake. We could easily have got a loan, and if we had done this, we might have grown the business quicker, because we could have hired extra staff, which would have generated more profits.

When you want to start a business, the most important aspect you need to think about is the financials. Often people don't pay enough attention to this. Gavin and I ignored them for a long time. After Chris joined the company, the first item on his agenda at meetings would be finance.

Before starting your business, look at what your competitors are doing. Think about how you could do something better or what you can offer that they don't do. I had good relationships with some of the energy suppliers and would regularly ask them what my competitors were doing and who was doing well.

Another important part of business is networking. If you make the effort to attend events, you never know who you might meet or what might result from them. If I'd not gone to Cheltenham Racecourse that time, I'd never have met Andy Blake, who introduced me to Chris. I always found supplier relationship days useful for the business. Once people had had a few drinks, it was easier to talk to them about ideas.

Another time, I went to a golf day with Crown Energy and met Mark Gamble, who was sales manager at the utility-switching company Make It Cheaper. He told me he lived in

Peterborough, which is half an hour from Corby. I kept in touch with him, thinking that one day I could see him working for Utility Bidder. One evening, Chris and I had a meeting with him in a restaurant in Peterborough and we offered him a job looking after suppliers. He's now head of operations.

Going to events can sometimes feel like a waste of valuable time, but if you go to the right ones, and you go to enough of them, they can pay dividends in one way or another.

I always wanted to be the best. If we were struggling, and other brokers were too, it didn't matter to me. I just wanted us to be the best. When Chris joined, he asked everyone at a meeting of the heads of department where they wanted the company to be in five years. I said, 'I want us to be the biggest, the best, and the most profitable.' Chris said this was possible.

You need to keep pushing yourself and never become complacent. When I'm at the gym, I'm always trying to push myself further, by lifting heavier weights or getting faster on the rowing machine. Business shouldn't be any different.

Stick with what you know works and the results will come. Self-doubt is something that affects us all. You have to keep faith in yourself and your ability. Someone once said that the more times you get told 'no', the better, because you are one closer to a yes. In football, if you're a striker and you're not getting goals, you have to keep making those runs and putting the effort in. Eventually, the goals will come. Understand that persistent effort often surpasses innate talent in achieving long-term goals.

A lot of people who go into business give up when they hit obstacles. You have to find a way around the obstacles and, where necessary, learn to adapt. Some people who lost their businesses during Covid blamed the virus. If you hit a crisis, you have to see it as an opportunity, not a problem.

Some businesses made a lot of money during Covid. There are always winners and losers in a crisis. You should always strive to be a winner.

If your business starts to grow, then you will have to hire people to do various tasks. At Utility Bidder, I actually wanted people with no experience, because we could mould them. And the likelihood was that if they were any good, they would stay. Sometimes people with experience bring with them bad habits or think they know better, and they will quite happily leave to go to a job that offers them a little bit extra. Whereas with people you bring in and train, they know you have given them an opportunity, and will stay with you. In most cases they would feel a loyalty to the company and that they were part of a team.

If you run a business, it's important to know what you're good at and what you're not, and then bring in the right people who can complement your skills and take on the areas that you struggle with. Don't expect to be able to do everything in a business. That's why I brought Chris in to take Utility Bidder to the next level. He had skills and knowledge that I didn't have. There were times in the early days of Utility Bidder when I didn't have a clue what I was doing, and as a result made mistakes.

What's equally critical is that you need to have the right kind of people around you. Otherwise, you can get into a mess, especially where finance is concerned. Sally and I made a good team. She was incredibly organised and took care of all the admin. I just wanted to sell. If I'd had the right people when we were growing as a business, and if Chris had joined earlier, then I think we could have become three or four times bigger.

Some of the mistakes I made were hiring the wrong staff. I hired some people who talked a good game but turned out to be rubbish at what they did. For instance, some people couldn't handle working in sales, because of the pressure. We had lots of issues with staff at Utility Bidder. You'd have someone who hadn't sold anything for a month and was moaning about their wages, and they'd be looking at sport on the BBC website instead of being on the phone. At one point, I banned staff using mobile phones in the office.

Another issue was dress codes. I always went to work dressed smartly. But trying to get some of the staff to do this was a battle. Some would arrive at the office looking terrible. My minimum requirement for the guys was trousers and shirt. I didn't ask them to wear a tie. There were a few occasions when I had to tell female members of staff that what they were wearing wasn't really suitable for work. We had dress-down days on Fridays. Some of the staff wanted permanent dress-down days. If someone was bringing in a million pounds a year in sales, then they could have a dress-down day every day, but until that happened, the dress code still applied. However, one of the reasons it was difficult to enforce was that Gavin would arrive at work sometimes looking very casual. As far as he was concerned, he could dress any way he wanted, as it was his business. I felt that, as the owners, we should set an example.

In any business, you utilise the staff to get what you want. At Utility Bidder we gave those we employed a good income, rewards and incentives.

A major incentive for the sales team was being allowed to go home early on Fridays if they had hit the targets. However, in order to leave early, some of the staff made out they had completed sales when they hadn't. And allowing sales staff to go home early on Fridays caused friction with staff in other departments. Success in a company is a collective effort. It's not just down to one group of individuals. Everyone has their part to play.

Another problem was that we tended to treat our sales team like superstars. As a result, some of them thought they were better than other members of the company and they could get away with anything they wanted. I let some people misbehave because their sales figures were good. Perhaps I shouldn't have allowed this; in some cases I should have fired people. Banter and having a laugh are fine, but you should only do this when you are winning. Some of the staff would be messing around when our sales were low. I found this very frustrating.

When members of the sales team were failing to sell, it was usually because they hadn't stuck to the script or the FAQs. For example, if one of the sales team asked a customer if they would like to save money on their energy bills and the customer said no, we needed to have an answer for that. We always tried three times before we let them put the phone down. The sales team were told not to give up with a customer until they were told 'no' three times.

We always tried to improve the way the sales team sold by getting each member to listen back to their calls. By law, we had to record the calls. No one liked listening to themselves on the phone. If someone had made a great call, I'd play it at the team meeting, so everyone could learn from it.

To be good at sales, you have to be friendly, talkative, show an interest in the customer – maybe by asking them how their weekend had been – try and identify how they like to be spoken to. You also have to be professional, but be able to switch to something a customer wants to talk about – say a TV programme or football. The aim is to build a rapport with them.

Being rejected by customers is hard, and it's easy to get discouraged, but you have to persevere. It's a good idea to listen back to your call to see what you said. You might have not stuck to the script or inadvertently annoyed a customer with something you said.

We had three superstars in the sales team. They could do a million in a year each. I was always asking myself how I could find more people like them. They were hungry to earn £100,000 a year, they didn't take no for an answer, they were thick-skinned and they knew how far to push customers. Other members of the sales team wanted to be like them because they wanted to make the same type of money.

We had call stats and sometimes I'd discover that someone had only spent one hour in an eight-hour day on the phone. I couldn't understand how that was possible. We tried 'power hours' where everyone had to stand up and only make calls. I'd clap my hands and say, 'Okay, guys, let's get the office buzzing.'

One of my main tasks was to keep staff morale up. I always tried to be positive about things, even if behind the façade I was consumed with worry. For example, if sales weren't going well, I'd say, 'Look, we've been here before, and we always manage to turn things around. So long as we do everything we're supposed to do, the results will come.'

As a leader, you have to be aware of what's happening among your staff. If you read autobiographies of top football managers, you see that they know when to put an arm around a player and when to kick them up the arse. Some people react well to a kick up the arse; others don't.

You should always try and create a culture of improvement. To help the staff improve, I brought in Lee Croucher, who ran a training and coaching company. He started doing annual appraisals, initially with the sales team and then with other members of staff. This started to create a culture of account-ability and personal growth within the team.

He taught the sales team how to identify the different types of people they encountered and how to adapt their sales pitch. He said customers could be classified by colours defining their motivation: blue people, who struggle to make decisions – therefore the sales team could influence them from a helping others point of view; green people, who need all the information and time to make informed decisions after a period of analysis; and red people, who just want to feel important and as if they have a deal no one else can get. Understanding what kind of person they had on the phone enabled the team to focus their pitch and get results.

We also tried gamification, which is where you try to turn work into a game. Different departments had different ways of earning points. This was easier to do with the sales team than other departments. We tried to make it fair to everyone, but it wasn't easy. We did a game based on the TV show *Deal or No Deal,* where someone who had performed well during the week would sit in the hot seat. We also had a game with a three-digit code on a lock. If someone guessed it correctly, they could win a grand. As well as these activities, we had a big raffle at the end of the month for the sales team. The more deals someone did, the more raffle tickets they got. If you did a one-year deal you got one raffle ticket. If you did a five-year deal, you got five raffle tickets.

Investing in the personal and professional growth of your staff pays dividends for a company. We ran NVQ courses as part of staff development and learning. The subjects included sales, administration, marketing and IT. The courses were held in-house. We did a graduation ceremony at the Christmas party and gave out certificates and awards. This was all about making the staff feel valued and giving them a sense of achievement. I wanted them to feel the company was a family. We called it Team UB.

Business Energy Consultants and Utility Bidder have employed hundreds of people over the years. In the early days, we'd just give people a copy of the *Yellow Pages* and a script and tell them to get on the phone. I've often wondered about those who left – whether it was their fault or ours. Maybe we didn't provide enough training. If we had, would they have stayed? It's impossible to know.

Because of reality TV shows such as *Love Island* or *Made in Chelsea*, and the rise of Instagram, some people think they can be an overnight success, making a lot of money without putting in the hard work. With really successful people, you don't see the work they've put in in order to get where they are. You just see the tip of the iceberg. When I drove taxis, people couldn't understand why I was working on Christmas Day. I couldn't understand why they weren't working. I earned good money on Christmas Day. There's no easy way to achieve success. The only place where success comes before work is in the dictionary. You do things others won't, so you can do things others can't.

I sometimes think Utility Bidder should have done better. At other times I think we did incredibly well. Since selling the company, I've wondered if I was really that good at running a business. Was it just luck? Was I just in the right place at the right time? And could I do it again?

The answer to all of these questions is the same: I don't know.

18

ROOTLESS

DESPITE MY RESERVATIONS about having sold Utility Bidder, the deal was done and I couldn't undo it. The big question now was what to do with the rest of my life.

Of course it was nice to have the money, but I missed all the day-to-day work. It gave my life a focus. The RAF had given me a focus; so had being in prison. After I was released, my focus shifted to starting a business and making it successful. I had done that, but having achieved it, I had thrown that focus away.

I was – and still am – involved with Utility Bidder. I sit on the board, attend monthly meetings with Sovereign and keep in touch with suppliers. I go into the office one day a month, but all I do is walk around and say hello to everyone.

I have more time to think about things now, which can be a good or a bad thing, depending on how you look at it. In the old days, I'd get up, go straight to the office, go to the gym in the middle of the day and leave the office at six. For relaxation, I'd go to a spa or sauna, play golf or watch Leicester play. I was busy twenty-four-seven. Now, I go to the David Lloyd gym and play tennis, but it's not enough. I miss the buzz of being in the office and doing deals. This is what it must be like for sports people or pop stars when they retire. And it's why football managers such as Sam Allardyce and Roy Hodgson carry on into their seventies. They could be sitting on a beach somewhere, but they don't want to: they'd probably be bored. It's the same for Rod Stewart. I saw him perform at Caesars Palace in Las Vegas in 2023, when I took seventeen Utility Bidder staff and my mum and dad there. He's had a residency at that world-famous venue for over ten years, and he's still putting on high-powered shows at the age of seventy-eight. I may be wrong, but I don't think it's because he needs the money.

When business decisions need to be made, I'm pretty good at taking them. But when it comes to my personal life, I'm not. I tend to leave things or let them drift. This may well have been what happened with Sally and me. Our relationship ended not long after the earn-out with Sovereign had been completed. I left our house in Church Langton and moved in with my brother Tom. Then he had to sell the house that he and his partner owned after their relationship broke up, so I bought a three-bedroom semi in Market Harborough into which he and I moved.

Without any commitments at the office, I can travel any time I want. While I'm not a big spender when it comes to cars and the like (as I say, I've only ever bought one new one), I love to travel, especially if it involves sporting events. Over the years, I've had some amazing experiences and rubbed shoulders with more than a few famous names. I've had my photo taken with Amir Khan at an open training session before his fight with Luis Collazo in Las Vegas; with West Indian cricket legend Viv Richards on a golf course in Antigua; and with rapper and Black Eyed Peas founder will.i.am in the private box that British Gas offered me at the Champions League Final at Cardiff in 2017.

I seem to spend more and more time in Tenerife, which is a four-and-a-half-hour flight from East Midlands Airport. After Sally and I broke up, I went there for a few weeks to try to get my head in order. The reason I like the island so much, apart from the sunshine and the great restaurants and bars, is that there's a real focus on sport and fitness there. Lots of professional sportsmen and women and national sports teams go there to train. The majority of tourists in Tenerife are British, although a lot of Scandinavians come in January and February.

I usually go to the bars and restaurants around Playa de las Vistas. I'm a regular at a couple of restaurants there. The waiters greet me at the door and never serve me food with lots of oil because they know I don't like it. In the evenings, I sometimes go to the Dubliner, which has live music. Most days, I'll go for a run along the beach, listening to the *Rocky* soundtrack on my headphones, and go swimming and spend time in the gym lifting weights. I've worked with tennis and golf coaches on the island and also with a physio. I always feel great if I'm in Tenerife.

One year, I flew some of the staff to the island for a week, as a reward for all their hard work. I took them out on a boat to see whales and dolphins. Sally took the girls to a water park, and we went to a restaurant where they only serve vodka by the bottle, which is brought to you decorated with sparklers. The trip was also about marketing, because everyone would put photos of the week on Facebook or Instagram, saying what a brilliant time they'd had. I hoped this might encourage their friends to ask about working for Utility Bidder.

I've considered living on the island, but the property market there has gone crazy since Covid, thanks to the growing number of 'digital nomads' renting rooms for a few months and working on their laptops.

I also go to Dubai several times a year because I've got friends there. The first time Sally and I went there, when I was trying to get involved in the property market, I wasn't that keen on the place. Over the years, though, it's grown on me.

On a trip to the Gulf to watch England play in the 2022 World Cup in Qatar, I stayed for some of the time at the Hilton Hotel in Dubai, where Ally McCoist, Ian Wright, Graeme Souness and other TV football pundits were staying. One evening, I was sitting in the bar when I realised Harry Kane was at the next table. I went over to say hello, only to discover it wasn't Harry Kane; it was his brother, Charlie, who was the spitting image of him. I apologised for my mistake. Charlie just laughed and said it happened all the time. It turns out that he's Harry's agent.

A year earlier, when I was staying with Paul Glass in his Dubai villa, he introduced me to Gary Hurley, a professional golfer who'd had some issues with his game and was on the verge of quitting after the Turkish Airlines Open in 2019. In 2015 he had been tipped as the next big thing in Ireland, after he steered Great Britain and Ireland to victory at the 2015 Walker Cup at the Royal Lytham & St Annes Golf Club. Paul told me he had agreed to provide him with some sponsorship for the season and that he was looking for additional sponsorship.

'Paul said you're looking for sponsorship,' I said to Gary.

'Yeah, that's right,' he replied.

'Tell you what, I'll sponsor you.'

'You will?'

'But only if I can be your caddie.' I was half-joking.

'Okay, deal,' he replied.

'Seriously?'

'Sure. I need a caddie.'

At that time, Gary was preparing to go on the Alps Tour in Egypt, but there was little prize money in it. To get promoted to the Challenge Tour, you had to finish in the top five or win three events in the season.

When Gary was due to take part in the Saudi Arabian Open qualifier at the Abu Dhabi Golf Club, I flew to Abu Dhabi to meet him. I had to be up for breakfast at 5.30am and meet Gary on the course. Players in the tournament would tee off at anywhere between 7.30am and 11am. A round was four-and-a-half to five hours, and I had to carry a large, heavy bag in heat of twenty-five to thirty degrees. It was hard work. Gary liked his clubs in the right place and wanted me to stand three or four yards to the right of the ball. He used a TrackMan – a radar system that can track and record the 3D characteristics of a sports ball in motion. A real caddie would have studied a map of the course and known everything about it, but I was a just novice; I was literally just a bag carrier. We'd have lunch and then afterwards, Gary would go to the range to practise.

Over a drink in the clubhouse, I asked him why he'd considered giving up golf. He opened up to me about how he'd hit rock bottom and felt directionless.

'I'd fallen out of love with the game,' he said. 'It was a really tough time. I didn't know where to look, where to go, what to do.'

'That must have been tough, mate.'

'Jesus, you know, I felt I didn't know how to play any longer.'

'So how did you rediscover your form?'

'Because I met Ed Coughlan.'

The name meant nothing to me.

'He's a performance coach,' Gary explained. 'He completely changed my life.'

'Really? How?'

'He made me feel safe. More importantly, he made me feel it was okay to feel the way I did. He said, "Where you are right now is okay." He helped me make peace with that. At that time, I was beating myself up, thinking, "I'm better than this. I know I'm a better player than this. Why am I playing so shit? Why am I struggling so much?" Like I say, I was going through a really tough time.'

Gary told me that after meeting Ed, he stopped playing golf for a few months. He would then meet Ed a couple of times a week on the golf course to discuss his life and his approach to golf. Ed gave him various exercises to do, and gradually Gary regained his self-belief. He had ended up developing a more positive mental attitude, but it had been a painful time.

Gary then had two tournaments at Sokhna Golf Club, on the Gulf of Suez in Egypt. He didn't play particularly well on the first day. I wasn't sure whether or not to say anything to him when he played a bad shot. He talked himself through every one. 'So, it's 140 yards, the wind's slightly off to the left. That's a three-quarter nine iron.' I'd stand there thinking, *He needs a nine iron*, and then he'd walk over to me and he'd ask for a nine iron.

After he came off the course, he said to me, 'I'm going to do my own bag tomorrow.'

'Okay,' I replied, surprised.

'I just need to be in control of everything I can be in control of.'

'You know, whether you push the trolley or I push the trolley isn't going to make any difference to your golf game.'

'I feel it will be better for me if I do everything myself.'

When he said this, I had already been wondering if caddying was what I wanted to do for a whole year. As I'd discovered, it's hard work: you're up at six in the morning to go to the range, you have lunch after five hours and then you return to the range. And golfers are really boring to be around; they're in bed at ten o'clock every night. As for me, I wasn't sleeping. To keep costs down, Gary and I were sharing a room. I would lie there thinking, *I need to have my own room at least.*

My daughter Hannah flew out to Cairo to spend a few days with me. I was on the golf course with Gary when I spotted her coming towards me. Gary signalled to her with his hand not to come any nearer. However, Hannah, thought he was just giving her a friendly wave, so she smiled and waved back, continuing to walk towards us. Fortunately Gary found it hilarious. I hired a tour guide, who picked up Hannah and me at the hotel, and we visited the pyramids, the Egyptian Museum and went on a camel ride in the desert. It was great to be able to spend time with her.

Gary's had mixed fortunes since I first met him. Gratifyingly, he's said in interviews that without the help Paul and I gave him, he wouldn't have got to where he is today. It may not look it, but golf is a tough sport to play professionally. Although travelling around the world to play the sport you love may sound like a dream come true, the reality is much tougher. You have to cope with a huge amount of pressure when you're in a tournament, and one mistake can cost you enormously. And golfers need to earn enough prize money in a season to pay themselves a salary and pay for hotels, travel and all the other costs – hence our shared room.

One time when I was telling Gary how directionless I

felt since selling Utility Bidder, he suggested I should speak to Ed Coughlan. I duly had a few phone calls with Ed, and talking to him, I realised it was too easy for me to disappear to somewhere like Dubai or Tenerife. He said psychiatrists just put plasters on things, whereas he ripped off bandages and wanted to see blood spurting. We talked about imposter syndrome. Was I really that good at business? Was it hard work that brought success? Or had I just been lucky? We also talked about various experiences I'd had in the past.

When I flew back to Dubai from Egypt, I went to the Ukrainian embassy. I'd read about guys from all over the world volunteering to help Ukraine fight Russia, and I thought perhaps I should sign up. However, no one at the embassy was able to tell me what I needed to do to enlist as a volunteer. Looking back now, having seen the horror and suffering Russia's invasion of Ukraine has inflicted, I wonder what on earth I was thinking.

Currently, I'm working with a couple of other energy companies. I've considered buying a few small brokers with a view to growing them and then eventually selling them. As that suggests, I'm probably more of an investor than an entrepreneur now. I've put money into: a home security company that Doug established in Ohio; the Lakes Distillery in Cumbria; a business involved in the cannabis extract CBD; a second-hand luxury car business; and WINIT365, the gaming software provider and developer of an online version of mahjong, the traditional Chinese tile-based game of skill and strategy. I've also provided loans to property developers. Virtually every day, I have someone asking me to invest in their company or project. In most cases, I say no.

Over the years, I've been involved in the property market. What began as dabbling has turned into a portfolio of forty properties. Perhaps I got involved in property because I never really enjoyed the energy industry and was always looking for something different to do. I buy flats or houses cheaply and then rent them out, and my mum takes care of the management. I bought a house for £167,000 from someone I knew who had negative equity. Today it's worth £310,000. I bought another property from a friend who was going through a divorce and couldn't afford the legal fees to sell it. I paid £102,000 for the house plus the legal fees. It's now worth around £230,000. In 2016 I bought three properties cheaply in Corby, and they've since doubled in value.

At a property seminar I attended, I met a guy called Ranesh, and we discussed going into business to buy land or property. We looked at large sites in London, Birmingham and Lubenham, just outside Market Harborough, where the builder had gone into administration. However, for one reason or another, we never pursued either sale. In 2018 I set up a property company because of the changes to mortgage tax relief. Prior to this, my properties were in my own name. When I eventually sell them, I expect to make a decent profit. Bricks and mortar is still one of the safest places to invest your money.

Buying property is a sideline and just somewhere to put your money. One of the messages of *Rich Dad Poor Dad* is that poor people spend their money, whereas rich people buy assets. It's a useful thing to remember, even if you're earning a lot and don't consider yourself poor. I know people who have earned £100k plus for several years and then hit financial problems. Because they'd spent everything they earned, they had to resort to credit cards or even sell their home.

I've continued to run the Wellandon tennis tournament. In 2021, I invited former Leicester City manager Micky Adams, who had become technical director of the Brook House

College Football Academy, to present the awards at the Square Bar in Market Harborough. He was brilliant. He talked about his time as manager of Leicester, including the incident where nine players were arrested for allegedly sexually assaulting German tourists in La Manga in Spain, and three players – Paul Dickov, Frank Sinclair and Keith Gillespie – were charged with rape. Micky said he had stood by the players because he believed they were innocent. The only thing they had been guilty of, he said, was being drunk. He spoke about his worries that his career at Leicester might be over. It later transpired that all the allegations against the players were false. I admired Micky for having the courage to do what he did.

I'm still a director of Corby Town. I lost interest in the club for a while, as there always seemed to be problems of one sort or another that needed to be dealt with, and the fans always seemed to be moaning. However, I regained my interest, and I'd like to think I've played an important role in keeping the club going. We finished seventh in the Northern Premier League Midlands Division in 2023 and eighth in 2024. At the time of writing (early 2025) we're second in the division and hoping for promotion.

Despite all my ongoing activities, there were days when it felt like there was nothing to get up for, and I stayed in bed late. I became conscious that I don't have enough structure in my life and I feel rootless. When I returned to the UK after spending seven or eight weeks in Dubai during the World Cup, and also travelling around Vietnam with my daughter, it was minus six degrees. The inside of my car was frozen. I thought, *I don't need to be here.* I could live anywhere in the world. Obviously, having plenty of options as to where you live and how you could spend your time is a great luxury. But sometimes having too many options can also do your head in. Wherever I put my energy, I came back to the same conclusion: I didn't know what I wanted to do with my life.

Whenever I was down, I kept thinking that I shouldn't feel like this. Many people are struggling to pay their bills and others are living through the kind of violence we've seen in countries such as Syria or Ukraine. Money may not make you happy on its own, but it allows you to buy all the things you want. Most people would love to have the kind of life I have. My problems seemed trivial in comparison with most people's.

I sat down at the start of 2023 to write down a list of goals and targets, but I couldn't think of anything. I considered setting set up another energy company. But it wouldn't be the same as when I set up Utility Bidder. I'd be more like a chairman or an investor; I wouldn't be hands on. Sometimes, I felt I should be trying to make more money and I felt guilty when I wasn't. Throughout my life I've always thought about investing for the future. But when is the future? Maybe the future's now.

I often think that had I not picked up Gavin that night in Market Harborough in my taxi and started accompanying him in Leicester, trying to persuade restaurant owners to switch their energy suppliers, none of my success would have happened. But someone else played an important role too. I think back to the chats I used to have with Beejay at North Sea Camp. He was the one who motivated me to go into business. I lost touch with him not long after I started Spotty Dog. Because he was desperate for cash after coming out of prison, I'd put him down as an additional card holder on one of my credit cards. However, he failed to pay back the money he'd borrowed on the card, and I had to pay it. I never heard from him again.

A few years later, I boarded a train to go to London to watch Leicester play Chelsea. To my surprise, at the end of the carriage, I saw Beejay. I could see from his behaviour that he was drunk. Part of me wanted to thump him and part of me wanted to hug him. In the end, I decided that, given the state he was in, it was probably better not to speak to him. I sat there thinking about some of the chats we'd had walking around North Sea Camp, and how he'd inspired me to take the plunge and set up the taxi business. When the train reached Bedford, I looked out of the window and saw Beejay being escorted along the platform by several station staff.

I'd never have met him in the first place, of course, if the incident with the taxi driver hadn't happened. I paid the price for my moment of madness.

Recently, I came across a letter from Phil, the guy I'd known at North Sea Camp. He wrote to me after his release to try to encourage me. He said, 'Just think, if you do extremely well, you could be saying for the rest of your life that one of the most fortunate things that ever happened to you was being sent to prison.'

He was absolutely right.

19

A PURPOSE AT LAST

ONE EVENING IN 2023, I was searching randomly on Google, continuing my quest to find an idea that might give me a purpose in life. I came across a retreat centre called New Paradigm, just outside Chiang Mai in Thailand. According to its website, the centre focused on mental health, trauma, anxiety, depression and burnout. It offered something called the eight domains programme, which aimed to help you improve various aspects of your life – emotional, physical and professional. I'd never been on a retreat before, and once upon a time I'd have run a mile from a place like this, but since I was feeling so direction-less, I thought it might be just what I needed. Even if I didn't get anything out of it, I'd have a fortnight in a hot country at a time when the weather in England was cold and wet.

So I emailed the centre, saying I was interested in the 14-day programme. A couple of days later, I had a Zoom call with Dirk Lambert, the centre's founder. After a brief chat, he said he'd send me a questionnaire to gauge what I was feeling about myself. He was as good as his word and I set about answering all the questions, realising I hadn't thought much about many of the topics listed. When I had a second Zoom call with Dirk, he said I'd scored 40 per cent. Someone who was feeling good about themselves, he explained, would usually score less than 20 per cent.

This result didn't surprise me: by now, I'd experienced bouts of depression on and off for several years. Dirk said he could book me into the centre the following week. I said that was fine, even though I was starting to get cold feet about going. When he emailed the following day to say that, unfortunately, he didn't have a space for that week, but he could definitely fit me in the week after, I felt a sense of relief. This was way outside my comfort zone, so maybe I should bin the whole idea. But after a couple of days, I thought, no, I'm going to go. It would be a new experience and I was bound to learn something from it. Sometimes in life, you just have to take the plunge into the unknown.

When I booked my flights, I decided to spend three days in Chiang Mai before going to New Paradigm. The country's second largest city, it's in the mountains of northern Thailand. I stayed in a five-star hotel near a historic Buddhist temple and spent much of the daytime doing Thai boxing in a gym and having tennis lessons. I felt relaxed and was enjoying myself, to the extent that I once more considered cancelling the retreat. I'd be quite happy spending the whole two weeks doing sport and just chilling out in the sunshine. But once again, I told myself I couldn't back out now. That would be the easy thing to do. It would be a challenge, but didn't I pride myself on never ducking challenges?

On the appointed first day, the centre sent a driver to collect me at the hotel. Within about half an hour, we arrived at New Paradigm, which was in the countryside just outside the city. Getting out of the car, I felt more apprehensive than ever. What would I do each day? Would I get bored? Who else would be on the retreat? I had no idea what I was letting myself in for. This could be one of the best experiences of my life, or a total disaster and a waste of money. And it really wasn't cheap.

The driver led me through a garden full of tropical plants and trees into a building, then down a corridor to a dining room. A woman cooking in an open kitchen smiled at me. On one of the walls was a whiteboard with a list of people's names and various activities alongside them.

Dirk, also smiling broadly, arrived to welcome me, motioning me to sit down. He briefly explained how things worked at the centre and told me that the lady cooking was his wife, who helped him run the centre.

'I think you're going to have a great time here, James,' he said.

'I hope so. I've never been anywhere like this before.'

'Most people who come here haven't. Just one thing. I need to explain that we ask our guests to hand over their laptops or phones.'

'Oh.'

'We don't want our guests to be distracted by the outside world, as this could impact how you experience the programme.'

'Okay, I get you.'

'The idea is to help you focus on yourself and not get distracted. After a few days, it won't seem strange.'

'No problem.'

'Don't worry; we put everything in a safe. On Sunday you'll be able to phone any close family members – but we ask you keep conversations brief – and you can check your emails.'

Understanding the principle, but with a definite sense of reluctance, I handed my laptop and phone over, wondering how the hell I would cope without them.

I would be staying in one of the chalets in the grounds. It was spartan but spotlessly clean. Once I had unpacked, I went for a Thai boxing session in the gym, followed by a swim in the open-air pool and an ice bath. At dinner, I was introduced to three other people doing the programme: a German software consultant of around my age, who was a digital nomad, flitting between the USA and the Far East; a female Belgian jockey who lived in Dubai; and an artistic Indian woman who, I later discovered, was battling mental health issues and a drug problem.

Each day of the programme was tightly structured. I got up at 5.30am and then went for a walk around the local area, which was mainly jungle. Before breakfast, you could have a sauna, go swimming or sit in the jacuzzi. After breakfast, I did yoga and meditation and then a one-to-one counselling session with Dirk. Following lunch, there would be some form of physical training, such as Thai boxing or aikido, then an ice bath followed by a workshop. You were given time to relax after dinner before lights-out at 9pm. It was not unlike an ultra-luxurious version of North Sea Camp.

The following morning, I meditated for the first time in my life. I had to sit on a mat in the garden with my legs crossed and eyes closed and keep totally still for twenty minutes. This was much harder than it sounds. Later, I sat down at a table in the garden with Dirk for my first one-to-one session. I'd read on the centre's website that Dirk had served in the Belgian army as a drill instructor and tank commander. After leaving the army, he had qualified as a systems engineer and set up businesses in Singapore, Vietnam and Thailand. He then became a psychotherapist and Buddhist monk. He'd also counselled a lot of US war veterans.

He asked me how I'd found the meditation.

Not easy, I confessed.

'Why do you think that might be?'

'I suppose because I'm used to being busy.'

'You know, meditation will make you more productive. It might sound strange that sitting still and doing nothing does this, but it's true.'

'Yeah?'

'Meditation helps you to recharge so you have more energy throughout the day. It also allows you to procrastinate less, and get more done in the same amount of time.'

'That's interesting.'

'You see, James, the basic idea of meditation is simple. Every time your mind begins to shift its spotlight away from your breath and you get lost in thought, you simply bring your attention back to your breath. And then you repeat this again and again.'

After a few days, I found it much easier to meditate, and I found that sitting still for twenty minutes had a calming effect on me. It helped me to focus more clearly on my life and think about what I wanted to do with it.

In one of my one-to-one sessions with Dirk, I talked about how I felt lacking in direction since selling Utility Bidder. He said he completely understood.

'Yeah?'

'Oh, absolutely. You know, before opening New Paradigm, I'd built up a number of retreat centres in Thailand, and they were very successful.'

'So what happened to them?'

'I sold them. And now I had all this money, but I didn't

know what to do with it. I mean, I bought cars and motorbikes – I love them – but something was missing. I thought, so what do I do now?'

'That's what I often feel.'

'That's why I opened New Paradigm. I needed to find some meaning in my life again. The reason I opened the retreat centres was to help people. To make a difference, if you like. And I think I'm doing that. I had all this money, but I didn't feel I was doing anything positive with it.'

'Having lots of money doesn't make you happy, does it?'

'No. Happiness doesn't come from what we have, but from understanding who we are and the gifts we have. It's about finding an inner peace. I think they understand this more in the East than in the West.'

Over the next few days, I kept returning to that conversation. Dirk seemed happy, which must be because he'd found his purpose in life. He was making a good living, but he felt he was helping people, doing some good. Ultimately, that was what I wanted to do. I needed to find something to do that would improve the lives of others.

Being away from my day-to-day life, and in beautiful and relaxing surroundings, I found it easier to focus more on my life. Dirk suggested I find my *ikigai*, which is what the Japanese call something that gives you a sense of purpose and a reason for living. In Japanese, *iki* means life and *gai* describes your value or worth. Under Dirk's guidance, I drew four overlapping circles and in each one I wrote a question: What do I love? What am I good at? What does the world need? How do I make money? The exercise was useful in helping me clarify aspects of my life. But, as I said to Dirk in our session the next day, I still hadn't found my purpose in life.

'Don't worry, James, you will.'

'You reckon?'

'Do you know what some of the most rewarding work I've done is?'

'Tell me.'

'Helping former prisoners of the war in Vietnam who developed PTSD. You can't imagine how satisfying that has been. I mean, some of these guys went through horrendous experiences.'

'I bet.'

'There are a lot of people out there who need help of one sort or another. The problem is that too often they can't find it.'

When my two weeks at the centre came to an end, I almost didn't want to leave. I felt much better about myself, and ready to start a new chapter in my life. But instead of returning to the UK, I flew to Tenerife. I thought that being there would make it easier to carry on the daily schedule I'd followed at New Paradigm, creating some much-needed structure. I spent the next month playing tennis, doing boxing, practising yoga and taking long walks along the beach.

I was sitting on the beach one morning in the sunshine, with the workbook I had made notes in at New Paradigm, and staring out at the sea, letting my mind wander. I kept coming back to that last conversation with Dirk when he talked about people needing help and not being able to find it. What could I do to help people? Should I set up a retreat centre similar to Dirk's? I knew that many people struggled to access mental health services. I quickly dismissed the idea, though, as I didn't have Dirk's background in psychology and spirituality, and I'd be way out of my depth. Perhaps I could do something to help people who experience energy poverty. This didn't really excite me. Then I thought about how my life had changed after being in prison. I was lucky to have been able to get my life going again. I had family and friends to support me, plus a determination to succeed. But what about those who come out of prison and can't get their life going again because they don't have any support or they're not in the right mental place?

From what I'd read, I knew the prison system in the UK was broken. You didn't have to be a rocket scientist to work that out. The system didn't seem to have changed much in the past two centuries. We still believe that the best way to treat many people who have committed crimes is to lock them up, often in overcrowded, filthy and crumbling Victorian buildings like HMP Leicester. Many prisons are understaffed and don't have enough experienced prison officers. The end result of the current system is that, for too many people, prison is just a revolving door or a conveyer belt of crime.

According to a House of Commons report, as of June 2023 the UK had a total prison population of approximately 95,526 people, the highest incarceration rate in Western Europe. The prison population of England and Wales has quadrupled in size between 1900 and 2018, with around half of this increase taking place since 1990. In 1900 there were 86 prisoners per 100,000 people in England and Wales. In 2022 this had shot up to 159 per 100,000.

If you commit a crime, you have to expect a punishment. But I don't believe prison is always the answer. Of course, people who are a danger to society need to be behind bars. But there are others who don't pose a threat to society. My North Sea Camp contemporary Gary Hart, who fell asleep at the wheel of his car and caused the deaths of ten people, received a lot of hate mail. *The News of the World* followed him around when he was let out on day release, complaining that he had only got six months for each person he had killed. But he didn't set out to kill any of them. Many of us have probably fallen asleep while driving; it happened to me lots of times when I was a taxi driver and when I used to drive down to Devon to see Hannah.

Government after government keeps putting sticking plasters on the prison system. Prison needs to be both a place of punishment, which is what losing your freedom is, but it also needs to be a place of rehabilitation. Some of the public just want retribution – for offenders to be punished – and they're not interested in rehabilitation. They say, 'Lock him up and throw away the key.' But ignoring rehabilitation just creates more crime, which those same members of the public don't want either. I've never believed that locking someone up in a cell for twenty-three hours a day, as I experienced in HMP Leicester, is going to achieve anything positive. You certainly can't rehabilitate someone if they're locked up all the time. All it does is lead many inmates to become depressed, suicidal or violent, either with other inmates or prison staff. Even if someone has committed horrific crimes, I don't believe that just locking them up does any good in the long term.

Was this my *ikigai*? Could I do something to help those in prison or after they were released? It felt possible. I didn't know what exactly, but I was convinced I could use my business knowledge and experience to benefit others. This might give me the purpose in life I'd been searching for.

For the first time in a long while, I felt excited.

20

'YOUR PRESENT STATE IS NOT YOUR FINAL STATE'

I READ ONE DAY that a new prison, HMP Fosse Way, had opened in Wigston, not far from me. Its focus was encouraging prisoners to learn new skills and gain qualifications before going back into the community. It had cost £286 million and been built on the site of HMP Glen Parva, which closed in 2017 and had been demolished. HMP Fosse Way was a category C resettlement prison. It was run by the private contractor Serco and could house 1,700 inmates. Among other things, prisoners were taught how to manufacture glasses for opticians and construct concrete components and lighting equipment that can be used in building future prisons. There was also a simulator where they could learn to drive construction vehicles.

This sounded like a genuine and imaginative attempt to make prison a place of rehabilitation, not just punishment. It seemed to be following the Norwegian prison model, which is regarded by many as the most effective and humane in the world. A BBC article in 2019 was headlined, 'How Norway turns criminals into good neighbours.' For example Halden Prison, the country's third-largest, has bar-free windows, dorm-style lodgings, fully equipped kitchens, Xboxes and a recording studio. The Norwegian system doesn't aim simply to punish. It treats prisoners like human beings and teaches them the skills necessary to become good citizens after they are released, so they stay on the straight and narrow. More emphasis is placed on rehabilitation than retribution. The approach seems to be working. Before Norway's prison reforms in the 1990s, the country had a reoffending rate in the range of 60-70 per cent. Today that rate (based on re-conviction within two years) is 20 per cent, the lowest in the world.

I decided to contact the governor at Fosse Way to see if he might be interested in my giving a talk. By sharing my story, I could perhaps help some of those in prison who lacked hope or didn't have any direction about what kind of work they might do after their release. I'm happy to say I got a good response. Wyn Jones, the governor (or prison director, as he is officially known), invited me to meet him at the prison the following week.

When I arrived, I wondered what I might be letting myself in for. I hadn't been in a prison since my release from North Sea Camp. Memories of my time there, and at HMP Leicester, came flooding back. In the glass-windowed reception, I was asked to hand in my mobile phone and watch, which were placed in a locker. Then I was finger-printed and guided through airport-style security, after which a prison officer led me down bright, clean and airy corridors, unlocking and locking doors as we went. The prison seemed quiet, unlike HMP Leicester, where there was always banging, screaming and shouting. Eventually we reached the governor's office.

Wyn greeted me warmly and said he was delighted to meet me.

'What do you think of our prison?' he asked, as I sat down in a comfy chair.

'It looks very different to what I expected.'

'It's a new model of prison. I've been in or around the prison service for nearly forty years. I started my career at Strangeways in 1983. That was a grim place. Fosse Way is nothing like that. We give prisoners decent conditions and provide opportunities to learn. This is a radical approach to cutting reoffending.'

He went on to explain that all the prisoners would be released within 24 months. Around 30 per cent of them were sex offenders. In other jails, such prisoners would be kept separate. But at Fosse Way they mixed with other prisoners. If a prisoner were to attack a sex offender, he would lose all his privileges.

I told him I really liked the emphasis on giving inmates skills to help them make a new start after prison.

He nodded. 'Our aim here is to help them get back into work once they finish their sentence. But tell me about you. I want to hear your story.'

I gave Wyn a brief overview of my life and explained that my business success would probably never have happened had I not been sent to prison.

He listened attentively. 'That's quite a story,' he said when I'd finished. 'You know, I was also in the armed forces.'

'You were?'

'The Royal Navy. I think there's a lot we could do together, James.'

I said I'd been wondering about giving a talk to the prisoners. 'You know, it might show them that even if you've been to prison you can still achieve things afterwards.'

'Absolutely. I'm all for this kind of thing.'

'Brilliant.'

One of the admin team then arrived to show me round. As we began the tour, she explained that inmates were housed in seven X-shaped four-storey blocks. Compared to most prisons, the corridors were shorter, with fewer prisoners on each wing, allowing frontline staff to see all cells and offenders quickly at any one time. Each inmate had a single room with a shower and a computer that allowed them to access training programmes, complete prison paperwork and order their meals from the canteen. The cells had ultra-secure, bar-less windows to help put an end to the smuggling inside of illegal drugs, phones and weapons. Prisoners could access prescription medication via vending collection machines operated with a thumb scan.

My guide proudly showed me a well-equipped gym, a library, classrooms, workshops and a barber's room, which, I noticed, was booked up for several weeks. There was also a coffee shop where prisoners learned how to be baristas. She then led me outside and showed me one of several astroturf pitches. She pointed to a building where other prisoners were learning to train dogs to become companions to the lonely or vulnerable.

'The inmates seem to have a lot of freedom,' I remarked, thinking that the prison felt more like a student campus or a hotel.

'The idea is that people will behave because they don't want to lose what they've got,' she said.

I told her that I'd spent time in prison after getting into a fight.

'Did prison stop you getting into more trouble?' she asked.

'No,' I said. 'That was when I was arrested in London after getting into an altercation with a guy at St Pancras Station.'

'Really?'

'Yeah. I spent six weeks worrying that I would end up in court and get sent to prison again.'

She opened the door to a carpeted room with a few empty desks.

'What's this?' I said.

'It's supposed to be a call centre,' she replied.

'Seriously?'

'But the company that was supposed to run it pulled out at the last minute.'

I thought a call centre where prisoners were taught how to sell would be amazing.

Everything at Fosse Way seemed to be genuinely geared to rehabilitating prisoners. Much thought had gone into it. True, it had cost a lot of money to build, but if it was successful it would *save* money by cutting reoffending rates. Even though it was surrounded by high metal fences and there were CCTV cameras everywhere, it almost felt like an open prison.

I reflected that if more money was spent on the kind of imaginative rehabilitation programmes Fosse Way provides, it would cut crime, make people and the streets safer, and cost less in the long run. If we provide more training and educational opportunities to those in prison, and for those who have been released, this will help reduce the chances of someone reoffending. If someone has skills, they can get a job. And if they can get a job, they are less likely to turn to crime.

As I walked back to my car, I felt excited by the prospect of sharing my story with the inmates.

A few days later, Wyn emailed me with a date and time for the talk. When I asked him how I should pitch it, he said, 'Just tell your story.'

I hadn't done much public speaking, and I'd never spoken

publicly about my life and going to prison. So what would I say that might possibly help the men there? They wouldn't want me just to talk about how I had rebuilt my life and become successful; they would want to hear how they could rebuild their own lives after prison and become successful too. I therefore needed to provide some takeaway lessons for them. I figured that a PowerPoint presentation would be more effective than me simply talking. Selecting the right images could help make my story come alive.

I spent ages working on my presentation. I had no idea how many prisoners would turn up, but Max, one of the prison officers, emailed me to say that fifty had expressed interest.

A few days before the presentation, I was at Corby Town's ground for a board meeting. The club had just signed a player called Rory McAuley, who had been sentenced in 2022 to four years in prison for possession of cocaine with the intent to supply. He had served two years. I got chatting to him in the board room. He said he got caught up in dealing drugs after his sister had been murdered by her boyfriend. When I said I was going to Fosse Way to give a presentation, and that I planned to work with inmates and former prisoners, he said, 'That's what I want to do too.'

'Yeah?' I said, surprised.

'I want to stop people from making the same mistake I made.'

'You never know, maybe we could do something together.'

I didn't sleep very well the night before my talk. I got up in the middle of the night and did some fine-tuning to the presentation, adding a couple more slides. In the morning, I added a section about the RAF and the importance of discipline, a bit about the trouble with the police I had been involved in, and how I understood what it was like to be separated from family, as I had found it difficult not being able to see Hannah.

I arrived at Fosse Way at around 4.30pm. The presentation was to take place in the resettlement unit and was due to begin at 5.30pm. A prison officer said there was a problem with the roll call, so it would be delayed. I was relieved, as I couldn't get my laptop to connect to the screen on the wall. I was beginning to panic. Fortunately, I had emailed Max the presentation earlier in the afternoon, and he arrived with his laptop.

By 5.50pm, no one had arrived and I was thinking that maybe only a couple of people would turn up. But then prisoners started to file in. As they took their seats, several eyed me with interest and a couple gave a friendly nod. By 6.10pm, between thirty and forty guys had arrived.

Looking at all the faces in front of me, I felt apprehensive. Would I manage to keep them engaged? Would they see my story as relevant to their lives? Would they switch off halfway through? I also felt a deep sense of responsibility to give these guys some encouragement and hope.

'Thank you for joining me today,' I began. 'My journey might seem unique, but it's a testament to the fact that no one is bound by their circumstances. From rock bottom in a prison cell to the boardroom of a multimillion-pound business, my life has changed dramatically. Today, I'll share how pivotal moments can lead to profound transformation and how the choices you make can redefine your future.'

I'd prepared thirteen slides, each representing a different part of my life. As each one came up, I read from my notes. When I reached the prison slide, I said, 'My most important takeaway from prison was that your present state is not your final state. Not if you don't want it to be and you're prepared to do what it takes to make that a reality.'

Nearing the end of my presentation, I talked about mastering sales skills. 'From dating to parenting and teaching, to choosing what to post online or how we dress, we're always selling – an idea, a version of ourselves, a belief. Master this and it might just be the way to unlocking success, however you define it, not just in business, but in life. It certainly was for me.'

I concluded by saying that everyone in the room was a blank canvas, fresh and ready for new beginnings. 'You're like a phone that's been reset to factory settings. It's completely up to you what you choose to install on it now. Remember the apps and content you choose can define your future. Time is our most precious commodity. This moment is truly a gift. They call it "the present" for a reason. Don't squander it. Make the most of this opportunity to reset. Thank you for listening.'

Applause rang around the room. The atmosphere felt electric. I then invited questions. Several prisoners asked how they could open bank accounts after their release and get credit. This is indeed a major stumbling-block for many people who have spent a long time in prison: it's hard to open an account if you have no credit history. One guy asked what it was like employing nearly a hundred people. I explained that it didn't happen overnight. When you set up a business, you might start employing one person, then a couple more, and then, gradually, you take on extra staff. It was over fifteen years before I found myself employing nearly a hundred members of staff.

Following the questions, I mingled with the prisoners. Two guys came up to me and explained that they had developed an idea for a project where inmates would mentor young people to prevent them ending up in prison. They called it ReachOut2StayOut. One of the guys revealed he had been given life for shooting a man dead as he drove his car. He had previously served time in prison for manslaughter after a shopkeeper was stabbed to death. The other said he had been sentenced to life for a joint enterprise murder when he went to a party in London with a group and a man was shot dead. I think the idea of convicting someone on the basis of joint enterprise is wrong. You could be with someone who pulls a gun or a knife on someone and have no idea that they were going to do so.

I admired what these two guys were doing. Talking to them reminded me that I too could have ended up in prison for murder had I not been pulled off the taxi driver that night. Alternatively, the taxi driver could have had a weapon, and I might have ended up dead. Both were chilling thoughts.

Another guy wandered up to me and said, 'I'm leaving prison in twenty-two days.'

'You must be happy,' I said.

'I don't want to end up inside again,' he said, shaking his head. 'No way, man. I want to go straight.'

'What did you do before prison?' I asked.

He shrugged. 'I've only ever sold drugs.'

I hesitated for a moment. 'Well, you can sell then.'

'I suppose so.'

'Perhaps that's what you should focus on.'

'You reckon?'

'Why not? What do you think you might do?'

'Someone's potentially got me a job in landscaping.'

'I mean, maybe you could become a landscape gardener and, you know, eventually start your own business.'

I wished that there had been more time to talk to him, but all the prisoners had to be back in their cells by 7.30pm.

As Max led me back to reception, he said he felt the presentation had gone down well with the guys, and he was sure that some of them would take something away from it. He mentioned that one of them was a rapper with millions of followers on social media. He had been transferred from a London prison to Fosse Way because people in his old jail wanted to have a pop at him.

Driving back to Market Harborough, I felt pleased with how the presentation had gone. There seemed to be a buzz in the room. I was keen to get going with my project for prisoners. But I could see that it might be more difficult than I'd first imagined. How would I feel about trying to help a sex offender go straight? Didn't they deserve a second chance? The truth is, I don't know what I would think about helping someone who had committed a rape or some other sexual offence.

What I do know is that I want to offer hope to those who are in prison or who have recently been released. That's why I gave my talk in HMP Fosse Way and, perhaps more importantly, that's also what this book is for. By breaking my silence to share my own life story – the details of which may shock many people who know me, so writing it wasn't an easy decision – I'm trying to show by example that better paths exist and crime isn't the only option.

We can all make a difference in life. You don't have to be someone, like me, who set up a business and sold it for millions. There are lots of small ways you can do something positive to help others. You could do a few hours volunteering each week or month, for example. I've chosen to help prisoners, because I have an affinity with them and I strongly believe we all deserve a second chance.

Dirk said to me before I left the retreat centre in Thailand, 'When we are no longer able to change a situation, we are challenged to change ourselves.'

One way we can change ourselves is to do something for others.

ACKNOWLEDGEMENTS

WRITING THIS BOOK has been a journey – one that has forced me to look back at the highs and lows of my life, the lessons I've learned and the people who helped shape me into the person I am today. I couldn't have done it without the support, guidance and patience of so many people, and I want to take this opportunity to express my gratitude.

Firstly, I want to thank Greg Watts, who worked closely with me as a ghostwriter, helping to shape my stories and experiences into something meaningful. Greg, your patience and ability to make sense of my chaotic memories made this book possible.

I would also like to extend my heartfelt thanks to Simon Edge and Dan Hiscocks at Eye Books. Their decision to publish my book was a pivotal moment, and I'm incredibly grateful for their trust, vision and support throughout this journey. Thanks also to Clio Mitchell and Dan Roberts for their work on the text.

To my family – thank you for being there through everything. From my early years in Market Harborough to the tough times and the celebrations, you've played an integral role in my life. Your support, even when I didn't always make things easy, has meant everything to me.

I would like to express my deepest gratitude to Sally, Bonnie and Robbie. Their unwavering support and dedication, especially during my time in prison, were invaluable. Their belief in me, and tireless efforts in helping grow the business have been a constant source of strength. I truly couldn't have done it without them, and I'm forever grateful for their support and commitment.

To my daughter Hannah – you are my greatest source of pride and motivation. Everything I do is with you in mind and I hope this book shows you that, no matter what obstacles life throws at you, you can always push forward.

To all of my friends who were part of my journey – thank you for the memories, the laughs and even the tough lessons. We may have had our fair share of wild moments, but through it all, I knew I could count on you.

To Gav – for climbing into that taxi that night and changing the course of my life. Who knows where I would be if things had gone differently? Sometimes, it's the smallest actions that have the biggest impact, and I will always be grateful for that moment.

And finally, to everyone who has supported me, shared in my journey or read this book – thank you. If my story can inspire even one person to push through their struggles and fight for a better future, then writing it was worth it.